Beyond the Walk:

The Secrets to a Calmer Dog, a Stronger Bond, and a Happier Life Together

Tim Jackson

Published by WriterMotive
www.writermotive.com

What Some of Our Clients Have to Say About Our Training and Behaviour Programmes

"When we adopted 17-month-old Beethoven, described to us as a 'hoolilab' we had no idea what a journey we would be on.... I would be on!! We've had dogs all our lives, we were not novices, but this beautiful chocolate Labrador was more challenging than we could have ever imagined. He was dog reactive on the lead in the very worst way. He didn't even bark, he screamed and dragged me to other dogs and their terrified owners. I started training in quiet streets in the dark. If I saw anyone I ducked behind hedges or cars....it was a nightmare, and I regularly came home in tears. I realised very quickly that I needed professional help. This was when I met Tim. Beethoven was untrained in every way so when Tim came to our home the dog went nuts.

Tim was so calm and assured me that Beethoven was merely excited, and we could work on that, he gave simple exercises I could work on for impulse control and settling. We went for a walk, Tim watched my beautiful dog and announced that he was frustrated and that's what the reactivity was, not aggression. He confirmed that my runs and walks weren't enough and he needed more exercise – off-lead exercise where he could run free! That was a terrifying prospect for me. Beethoven had already dashed into most of my neighbours' homes...and cars! He was wild and I felt out of control! But he was also gentle and loving, he adored the grandchildren and never ever knocked them over. My old Dad too, he was so gentle with him. He was a good boy; I just didn't know how to help him with his problems.

Tim was marvellous, confident, patient and kind. We had 1-1 training sessions where Tim helped me find tools that could help Beethoven engage with me rather than want to get to the other dogs. I'm the crazy lady who walked with 4 tennis balls and a bubble wand because I knew he would always come back for them.

I started to take Beethoven to Pets2impress once a week to socialise and enjoy all that this fabulous daycare has to offer. I joined Tim's online dog club The Sandancer Superhero Dog Club, the webinars and teleclasses were invaluable and still are. They help us to understand our wonderful canine companions and offer new insights into training. We learned how to start scent work, wow!! I had no idea how to do that, now we practice regularly with different scents and items, it turns out that Beethoven is brilliant at this and thoroughly enjoys it, so calming too! So I now had tricks to play with when we were walking, turning to break Beethoven's focus on other dogs, little scatter feeds when I felt unsure of dogs, 1,2,3.... a game-changer, just showing Beethoven his ball and letting him carry it. Simple things that made the world of difference to us.

Our club has monthly challenges which are always accessible and sometimes more challenging than others. Working with my boy towards those challenges is so much fun and so very rewarding!

We are a fabulous group and all support and encourage each other. Tim is always accessible and responds to any questions promptly…. what a support network we have!

I am delighted to say that thanks to all the advice, training and support, we have the most wonderful boy who shares almost every part of our lives, which is exactly what we wanted when we rescued this beautiful, crazy, and very challenging Labrador.

We got Beethoven in August 2021 and decided to return to South Africa in October 2024. Of course, Beethoven came with us and here he has a clean slate! No neighbours hiding from me, everyone just sees a beautiful, well-behaved, confident happy boy. I asked Tim if I could remain a Sandancer Superhero from afar, I feel all the new enrichment challenges, the monthly telecasts and support of Tim and my dear friends are invaluable in my journey with this dear boy of mine.

I have never known anything like Pets2impress, it is a very special concept with Tim's very knowledgeable support. I wish Tim all the success he deserves in all his new ventures!" **Elaine Coates**

"Our three-year-old west highland terrier wasn't responding well to our new shih tzu puppy. We'd expected jealousy etc., but he was really fearful and became aggressive, withdrawn and generally seemed depressed. He'd stopped playing with us, and we were getting to the point of returning our puppy.

Tim came out and spent some time with us and our westie. Of course, it was us that got the training, lol! Tim was brilliant and gave an honest assessment of our situation and changes we could make immediately, as well as training exercises we could do with the dogs.

After perseverance and practice, we now have two happy dogs and the confidence to continue with the work. I can definitely recommend Tim. Thanks so much for a happier life ." **Vicki Kenyon**

"I joined the Sand Dancer Club when it started a couple of months ago, and I am so pleased that I did. I have known Tim for a while now through puppy class, and some 1-1 training, and my dog loves daycare. The work that Tim has done with Murphy and the advice given has been fantastic. The most telling point for me, as well as seeing the improvements in Murphy's behaviour, is the fact that my dog, who doesn't easily trust people or want them to touch him, loves Tim and will always run over with excitement to greet him!

The Sand Dancer Club has lots of advice as well as lots of fun activities to do with your dog that build on focus and having a great relationship with your dog. For me, one of the best things is that the group is so supportive of each other, offering praise and suggestions when people ask for advice. Tim is always quick to respond to any questions asked. I really enjoy the question-and-answer live sessions as, quite often, the questions others have also result in activities that will help in lots of different situations.

I have enjoyed some really good online training through the Club, which was both fun and informative. Murphy and I love the monthly challenges and learning new things. We are really enjoying the benefits of being in the Sand Dancer Club" **Nicola Mackins**

"I have a one-year-old Red Cocker and was having a lot of problems with his behaviour — my fault as I totally spoilt him from day one. Tim was recommended by my dog groomer. I rang and booked a telephone consultation. I felt at ease as soon as I spoke to him. He was so lovely and made me feel positive from the start.

We got out of the programme everything we needed. It's up to us now to keep putting in the work we learnt.

After the first lesson, we saw a huge improvement in our dog's behaviour.

I would definitely recommend Tim and Pets2impress." **Sara White**

"We bought two puppies and found it extremely difficult to do anything with them; we needed help.

We got in touch with Tim at Pets2impress, who came and did an assessment. He informed us that they had fear-based aggression towards other dogs, and he put our minds at ease, knowing that there was something we could do to help them.

Without Tim's help, I could not have coped. I can't recommend Pets2impress enough ." **Mr and Mrs Selby**

"My partner and I adopted a dog from Europe. All was well until three months later when he started to show signs of aggression towards other dogs and men.

We contacted Tim for an assessment and booked him for training. We did everything Tim suggested, and now our dog can be around other dogs (even daycare) and people. We now have learnt the tools and techniques needed to recognise when our dog is in a situation he is not comfortable with, and we are able to use the training commands to get him out of it, which means no more aggression! Thank you, Tim." **Mr S Scott**

"I have a male dog called Storm, who is a Newfoundland cross bullmastiff and has an anxiety issue. He got to the point where he was very fearful of strangers and would growl and bark to scare them off. After several weeks of training with Tim and him bringing various people along to the house, Storm has now started to relax and is nowhere near as bad as he was. I will continue to use Pets2impress with Storm as I can't believe the results they are having with Storm. I am over the moon, and I can now actually start to relax. If you're thinking of using these guys, then it's money well spent." **Lee Brown**

"I have absolutely loved taking part in the online course. I love my time spent with Paddy, teaching him new tricks etc., and this course has opened up a whole new load of ideas that I can use and implement in our day-to-day activities that didn't even cross my mind. I thought it was going to be a real struggle for him during this isolation period with the lack of exercise and stimulation that he is used to on a daily basis. He is used to a good 2/3 walks per day as well as 2 – 3 full days at Pets2impress daycare, so naturally, I thought he would be bored during lockdown and bouncing off the walls with energy. During this course, his tail has never stopped wagging, and I've found that he is just as tired at night during this time as he was after a busy day on the go. Thank you, Tim, for everything you have done." **Samantha Heley**

"Having the resources from Tim at Pets2impress available through the lockdown has been invaluable. The changes and help provided have kept our puppy active, stimulated and happy! In a massive change to normal routine, my worry was that Cobie would suffer and lose the confidence that she had gained, but instead, she has learnt so much, and we have the knowledge to keep things going after this is over." **Amy McFaulds**

"My Black Labrador Charlie had an amazing time completing the online challenges in the Pets2impress 14-day challenge. He learnt a lot, and so did I. It was both fun and educational! I ordered him the isolation pack so he could get some toys and treats as a reward for his hard work. The pack gave me some more ideas on how to challenge him and train him too." **Anni Jowett**

"I would just like to say that Tim came to Stockton-On-Tees yesterday to see my Mam with her dog, Mavis. Tim has made my Mam feel that she can help Mavis, and my Mam isn't upset anymore now that she knows what she needs to do to help her. I'm so thankful for your help. I highly recommend this company; thank you so so much." **Victoria Ainsley**

"Thank you so much for all the advice and tips; we definitely have a better-behaved pooch, but still some training to be continued.
To think, just over a month ago, Dave and I were tearing our hair out with a pup who ruled the roost, and life was not enjoyable for any of us including Lara.
You have changed our lives, and since being introduced to you at a web seminar by Katie (Dogwood), the combination of training with yourself and Scentventure with Dogwood, we have a relaxed puppy who is so happy, and we are all enjoying being a family!
I honestly can't thank you enough, and I have already spread the word about Pets2impress to a couple of friends who are thinking of getting a dog.

We will continue our training and advice and keep you updated! Thank you again from all of us, we are finally a family!" **Charlotte and Dave**

"Thanks for all your help during lockdown. Training Maverick is a work in progress; we are learning a lot along with Maverick. All your ideas and techniques have been very useful, and we will continue to use them. Life during lockdown with Maverick has been a lot easier. We've had fun, and I think you have saved us a lot of stress. We are happy to recommend you." **Tracie and Stephen Cook**

"Excellent service. Trainer very knowledgeable and explained everything very clearly and showed us how to do training. Very fun sessions with very happy puppies and owners. Very highly recommended" **Cheryl Murray**

"We have been using Pets2impress since its inception. Tim taught our boys to walk on a lead, recall and how to behave as family pets. They've stayed with Tim when we have gone on holiday and loved it. They are walked during the day by Shannon, and I cannot recommend their services enough. Very flexible if you have to make a last-minute change and always happy to help if they can. You've tried the rest… now try the best" **Lesley Elliot – Burn**

"I've been a member of The Sandancer Superhero Dog Club with my 16-month-old Border Terrier Bronte since it started, and I can't recommend it highly enough. As with many dogs, Bronte has her own little quirks that make training without proper instruction sometimes quite difficult and stressful. Through the various webinars, games and trick challenges along with Q&A sessions, I am finally starting to really learn about what makes Bronte tick and really respond to me. I have seen such a huge improvement in Bronte's engagement with me when out on a walk, although we still have a way to go, particularly when there are other distractions about. I know that we will overcome the challenges because we have such great support and advice available to us. Tim provides such friendly and useful advice through his various channels, makes himself available whenever you need some additional personal advice, and the support from all the other club members really helps to inspire you to keep on working hard at the training. For me, the Club is a special family, and if you want both you and your dog to be the best that you know you are both capable of, the Club is definitely the Club to join" **Kate Henderson**

"I'd like to say that the course has been fantastic. Easy to watch, entertaining, and informative. I love the whole idea of engaging our dogs with games when actually out walking! I've always just walked my dogs (I do talk to them all the time tough!), I have

allowed them off-leash and had pretty decent recall. Enter Beethoven, and it's a whole new experience! I'm rubbish at the games in the house, mainly because my wee monster follows me everywhere. If I'm busy moving around, he's moving around with me. He only really rests when I do or if I go out!

My go-to with Beethoven off-leash has always been the tennis balls; they are his highest-value treat on a walk. I play the two ball throwing in different directions (can't remember the name!) now, and that really engages him! When I see other dogs or people, I call him back immediately (I find timing crucial!), and I've started playing various games, even funder* (see Pg 49), which I'd never thought of using on a walk! It works. He's only interested in me! Tossing the treats in the leaves or long grass, brilliant, he loves it! I have him spinning and sitting and bumping and just anything I can remember! Oh, and the fallen trees, he loves walking along them and jumping over! We've both been having so much fun, and sometimes, he's so tired or contented walking home that we can get past on lead dogs without drama....my nemesis!

I don't know if my waffling here is what you're looking for, but I would say that I found the course most inspiring, practical and simple to follow. I think the key is not to get complacent and stop working; keep the walks fresh and exciting! We can only get better and better. I do feel that when he fails, I've generally failed him first. I see that when I analyse a flop!!! We're not having so many, and I'm certainly much more confident when I go out now. I have a plan and tools to use." **Elaine Coates**

"We've really enjoyed Ready Steady Recall. The one-hour webinar each week has been ideal; it fits into the evening after work and has been ideal in that it allows us to practice the activities at our own pace. Your presentation style and humour have really made the course fun and easy to understand. The Facebook group has been very supportive, and it has been so easy to upload videos for feedback. We appreciate your fast response and valuable comments.

We feel we now have the tools and knowledge of how to use them; Archie is so focused on us while indoors; however, as soon as we cross the threshold to the outside world, he has a sensory overload, and we lose engagement. Over the past four weeks, we've definitely seen a massive improvement in Archie's engagement by playing the games outside the house. We need to take baby steps with him, but the improvement we've seen and the experience of completing this course has given us a way forward. We now feel much more positive that we will achieve our goal of enjoyable walks and great recall in the future." **Gill Vardy**

Contents

Mission Statement

My mission is to provide a safe, enriching, and joyful environment for dogs to thrive. I am dedicated to offering a holistic experience that fosters both mental and physical wellbeing through structured activities, personalised care, and a nurturing atmosphere. My enrichment programs, including scent work, agility training, and adventurous outings, are designed to stimulate your dog's natural instincts and promote confidence, happiness, and overall health. I believe in creating a community where every dog feels valued and loved.

Introduction

Back when I was younger, which seems like a long, long time ago now, I wasn't allowed to have cats or dogs. Shocking, right? No cats curling up in my lap, no dogs bounding around the house. Instead, I had hamsters and gerbils. Not quite the same, I know, but they were my introduction to the animal kingdom. I'll never forget my first hamster. His name was Hammy—not the most original name, but cut me some slack, I was a kid. Besides, Hammy didn't seem to mind.

Back then, hamster care was pretty basic. They got a tiny cage with a plastic house, some bedding, a wheel, and maybe a ball they could roll around in for exercise. Let's be honest, though: those hamster balls mostly resulted in Hammy smashing into walls and furniture. I remember reading about hamsters in the wild and how they loved to dig, forage, and explore. Pet hamsters, on the other hand, got none of that. So, I decided to spice things up for Hammy. I started making mazes out of cardboard boxes for him to navigate. For my gerbils, I created digging and burrowing areas, and I'd spend hours watching them work their magic. Little did I know, I was providing those little creatures with something called enrichment. At the time, I just thought I was being creative because, let's face it, we didn't have Xboxes to keep us entertained back then....I'll let you do the maths on my current age!

Speaking of creativity, I can't leave out the snail circus I set up in the back garden. Yes, you read that right. A snail circus. I commandeered the family tent for my masterpiece, much to my brother's disgust. While he had visions of us camping under the stars, I was busy orchestrating snail performances. I thought it was brilliant. He, not so much. Looking back, I realise those snails were probably just trying to escape my clutches, but hey, they got their five minutes of fame.

So although I believed myself to be a genius for creating these things enrichment, as it turns out, isn't a new concept and my maze-making skills certainly didn't make everyone thing oh we need enrichment for animals. Zoos have been doing it for years to keep their animals mentally and physically stimulated. From puzzle feeders for big cats to scent trails for bears, enrichment is about mimicking natural behaviours and improving an animal's quality of life. It's fascinating stuff. In fact, as I write this introduction, I've got a trip planned to Edinburgh Zoo to spend the day with their enrichment team. I'll be sharing all about that visit in a later chapter - let's hope you make it that far in the book!

Now, if you've read any of my other books, you'll know about my old dog, Lady. I could talk about her for hours. Lady was the reason I discovered my passion for behaviour, training, and—you guessed it—enrichment. She was a beautiful soul, but came with her fair share of challenges. Separation anxiety, training issues, you name it, we faced it. Things got so tough that I eventually sought help from a canine behaviourist. He visited my home, observed Lady, and gave me a list of things to work on. One of those things was providing more enrichment.

At the time, the word "enrichment" went straight over my head. My face must have been a picture of confusion. But I listened, took the advice, and started implementing it. And wow, what a difference it made. I saw a huge improvement in Lady's behaviour and overall happiness. Before that, I thought I was doing everything right. I walked her, fed her, and made sure she had the basics. What I hadn't realised was that I wasn't meeting her mental and emotional needs. I wasn't providing her with the opportunities to use her brain, instincts, and energy in meaningful ways. That was my lightbulb moment.

Lady's journey ignited a passion in me to learn more about animal behaviour and enrichment. I started working as a veterinary nurse and spent 14 incredible years in practice. Those years taught me so much, and I loved being able to share what I'd learned with clients. One of the most common situations we dealt with was post-surgery recovery. After neutering, the standard advice was 48 hours of rest followed by a week of strict lead exercise. Clients would call in a panic, saying their dogs were climbing the walls. That's when I'd step in with some basic enrichment ideas to help burn off their dog's energy in a calm and controlled way. It was rewarding to see the difference those simple activities could make and fear not my friend (we can be friends, right?) there is a chapter later in this book which goes into more detail regarding enrichment for dogs that need to rest.

The thing about enrichment is that it's not just about keeping animals busy. For it to truly count as enrichment, the animal needs to benefit from it in a meaningful way. It's about improving their wellbeing and allowing them to express natural behaviours. For dogs, that might mean sniffing, chewing, digging, or problem-solving. Every dog is different, and what works for one might not work for another. That's the beauty of enrichment—it's all about tailoring activities to suit the individual animal.

So, how much do you know about enrichment? I'm guessing you've heard of it before; otherwise, you wouldn't be reading this book. Maybe you're already incorporating some enrichment into your dog's life, or perhaps you're feeling a bit guilty because you're not quite sure where to start. Either way, don't worry—you're in the right place. This book is here to guide you, inspire you, and give you all the tools you need to provide your dog with the enrichment they deserve.

We'll be covering everything from simple, budget-friendly ideas you can try at home to more elaborate activities for those looking to go the extra mile. Along the way, I'll share stories from my own experiences and we'll also explore the science behind enrichment and why it's so important for your dog's mental, emotional, and physical wellbeing. Don't let the word science put you off, I'll keep things very simple, I promise.

By the time you've finished this book, you'll have a whole arsenal of enrichment ideas to draw from. More importantly, you'll have a deeper understanding of your dog's needs and how to meet them. Whether your dog is young or old, high-energy or laid-back, there's something in here for everyone. And who knows? You might even find yourself enjoying the process as much as your dog does.

So, let's get started. Let's dive into the world of canine enrichment and discover how it can transform your dog's life—and yours. Because when it comes to our dogs, they deserve nothing but the best. And trust me, seeing your dog's tail wag with pure joy as they engage in an activity you've created for them? There's nothing quite like it, well that's how I felt anyways when I started providing more enrichment for Lady and fingers crossed you will too.

Chapter 1
What is Enrichment?

When we think about giving our dogs a good life, the first things that come to mind are walks, food, and the occasional belly rub. But there's so much more to it. Dogs, just like humans, thrive when their minds and bodies are engaged. That's where enrichment comes in.

Enrichment is all about providing activities that stimulate a dog's mind and body while engaging their natural instincts—things like foraging, hunting, problem-solving, and exploring. It's more than just a physical workout; it's about meeting emotional, cognitive, and sensory needs too. Sure, a walk around the block is great, but it's only scratching the surface of what our dogs truly need to live fulfilling lives.

The Smithsonian Conservation Biology Institute defines enrichment as 'the process of providing stimulating environments for animals to demonstrate species-typical behaviours, exercise control or choice over their environment, and enhance their wellbeing.' Sounds fancy, right? But it boils down to one simple truth: dogs are happiest and healthiest when they're given the chance to think, play, and work.

The Benefits of Enrichment

Enrichment is a game-changer. It helps reduce boredom, which means fewer destructive behaviours (goodbye chewed-up shoes!). It improves mental wellbeing, supports cognitive health, and even boosts physical fitness. Perhaps my favourite benefit? It strengthens the bond between you and your dog. When you engage your dog in enrichment activities, you're not just giving them something to do; you're building trust, creating memories, and deepening your connection.

The Five Pillars of Enrichment

To truly enrich a dog's life, we need to consider the five main pillars of enrichment: sensory, intellectual, environmental, social, and physical. Each pillar meets a different need and contributes to your dog's overall wellbeing.

So let's look a bit more at what they are and how you can incorporate them into your dog's daily routine.

1. Sensory Enrichment

Dogs experience the world through their senses, with their incredible noses leading the way (be sure to check out the chapter 'How to Scentivate your relationship with your dog' later in this book). Sensory enrichment engages their sense of smell, sight, sound, taste, and touch, offering new and interesting experiences.

Simple ideas for you to try at home : Create a scent garden in your backyard or even in pots on your balcony. Use herbs like lavender, mint, and basil, and let your dog sniff to their heart's content. Indoors, try hiding treats around the house for a scent-tracking game. Both are very simple but offer so many benefits for your dog.

2. Intellectual Enrichment

The intellectual pillar of enrichment challenges a dog's brain and keeps their minds sharp. It's all about problem-solving, learning new skills, and engaging their curiosity.

Simple ideas for you to try at home : Teach your dog new tricks or offer puzzle toys that make them think to get a reward. Even something as simple as an empty cardboard box filled with treats and scrunched-up paper can be a fun brain workout.

3. Environmental Enrichment

This pillar focuses on improving your dog's surroundings. It's about creating spaces that are interesting and engaging.

Simple ideas for you to try at home : Set up a digging pit in your garden where your dog can dig for buried toys or treats. Indoors, you could rearrange furniture to create a little obstacle course or provide different textures for them to walk on, like rugs, mats, and towels.

4. Social Enrichment

Dogs are social animals, and social enrichment focuses on their interactions with humans, other dogs, and even other animals.

Simple ideas for you to try at home : Arrange safe playdates with other friendly dogs or spend time training and bonding with your dog. Even just sitting together and having a cuddle counts as social enrichment... permission granted to snuggle up on the sofa to sit and watch Netflix.

5. Physical Enrichment

Physical enrichment involves activities that get your dog moving. It's not just about burning energy but also about keeping their bodies healthy and strong.

Simple ideas for you to try at home : Try new games like tug-of-war, or take a walk in a different location to mix things up. You could even set up a mini agility course in your garden or living room.

Don't worry, my enrichment brain doesn't stop there. I will be providing a lot more examples in later chapters as we dive deeper into each pillar of enrichment.

First, let's talk about how these pillars of enrichment apply to us humans. One of my favourite places in the world is Beamish, the open-air museum. Beamish Open Air Museum, located in County Durham in the North East of England, is a living history museum that transports visitors back in time to experience life in the North of England during the 1820s, 1900s, 1940s, and 1950s. With its authentic buildings, working trams, and costumed staff, it offers an immersive and interactive glimpse into the past. From the bustling 1900s town to the serene countryside farm, Beamish provides a rich tapestry of experiences that capture the essence of bygone eras.

I take my kids there regularly, and it's not just a fun day out—it's a perfect example of how enrichment benefits us too. Here's how Beamish ticks all five pillars of enrichment for me and my family:

- **Sensory Enrichment:** From the smell of coal fires to the sound of steam engines, Beamish is a sensory wonderland. There's always something new to see, hear, and experience, whether it's tasting traditional sweets or feeling the textures of the cobbled streets underfoot.

- **Intellectual Enrichment:** Every visit teaches us something new. Whether it's learning about life in the 1900s, watching traditional crafts being made, or understanding how old machinery works, Beamish keeps our brains engaged and curious.
- **Environmental Enrichment:** Beamish offers a constantly changing environment. One moment, we're in a 1900s town; the next, we're in a pit village or on a farm. Each area is full of unique sights and experiences, keeping us engaged and excited. On my latest visit, there were two violinists playing in one of the old farmhouses, and they were teaching people a dance very popular from the late 1800s. Of course, I volunteered the children much to their dislike, but fear not dear reader, I captured their embarrassment on my phone.
- **Social Enrichment:** Visiting Beamish is as much about the people as it is about the place. From chatting with staff in period costumes to sharing laughs with some of the other visitors, there's a strong sense of community and connection. I have taken many people to Beamish for the first time and it never fails to impress. In fact, back in the day, Beamish was my go-to place to take lady friends for our first date... and they say romance is dead!
- **Physical Enrichment:** Let's not forget the walking! Beamish is huge, and exploring it means plenty of exercise. Whether it's climbing hills, wandering down the mine, or taking turns playing Booler in the old school playground, there is plenty to do to keep you physically enriched.

When I'm at Beamish, I can see how these experiences enrich my life, and it's a great reminder of how important enrichment is for our dogs too. Just like us, they need sensory stimulation, mental challenges, an engaging environment, social interaction, and physical activity to thrive.

Enrichment isn't just a buzzword; it's a way of life. It's about giving your dog—and yourself—the tools to thrive, not just survive. It's about creating a life filled with joy, curiosity, and connection. So, as you read on and learn more ideas for enriching your dog's life, remember: enrichment is a journey, not a destination. And trust me, it's one worth taking, just like a visit to Beamish is if you are ever stuck for a nice family day out.

Now, let's dive deeper into how you can make enrichment a daily part of your dog's world.

Chapter 2
The Canine Brain – How Dogs Learn and Why Enrichment is Essential

Enrichment is not just about preventing dogs from eating your sofa or giving them something to do while you enjoy a cuppa in peace. Enrichment is actually changing your dog's brain—and in a really powerful way, may I just add. So, let's get into the science of the canine brain, how dogs learn, and why enrichment is so crucial to their mental and emotional wellbeing. I promise to keep this chapter as simple as possible, but I do feel it is important for you, as a dog owner, to understand a bit more about how the canine brain works and the benefits enrichment can have on it.

A Healthy Brain – More Than Just a Thinking Machine

The canine brain is a high-energy organ, consuming 20% of the body's total energy. That's a lot for a dog that doesn't even have to think about tax returns or whether they left the oven on. But just like with humans, a healthy brain leads to a healthy life. When a dog's brain is stimulated in the right way, it builds connections that help them problem-solve, regulate emotions, and adapt to their environment. The healthier the brain, the more flexible and resilient the dog becomes.

But how do we actually understand what's happening inside a dog's head? Let's talk about Dr. Daniel Siegel's Hand Model of the Brain—a super simple way to visualise how the brain works.

Imagine your hand as a mini canine brain:

- **The fingers = Cortex :** This is where thinking happens. Decision-making, memory, planning, and problem-solving all take place here. If your dog is working out how to get a treat out of a puzzle toy, this is the part of the brain firing away.
- **The thumb = Limbic System :** This is the emotional control centre, responsible for what motivates your dog, what holds their attention, and how they remember things.

- **The palm = Brainstem :** This is the survival centre. It controls basic life functions like breathing, heart rate, sleep, and appetite. It's also responsible for reactive survival behaviours—so if your dog suddenly flinches or bolts when they hear a loud noise, that's the brainstem kicking in.

Now, here's where things get interesting. Dogs don't have the same cortical power that we do, meaning they don't overthink things the way we do (which is why they don't lie awake at night worrying about whether Karen at work secretly hates them). However, their limbic system—the emotional brain—is incredibly similar to ours. This means that their emotions are real, deep, and impactful. So, when a dog experiences fear, frustration, or stress, they remember it—sometimes forever.

How Dogs Handle Conflict (and Why Body Language Matters)

Dogs are a social species, meaning that communication is key to avoiding unnecessary conflict. If you've ever watched a group of dogs interacting, you'll see a lot of subtle signals—body language, eye movements, postures—all designed to defer conflict and avoid fights. This is because, in the wild, unnecessary fights are risky. A serious injury could mean death, so dogs have evolved ways to de-escalate tension before it turns into a full-blown scrap.

However, dogs are also a competitive species. If two dogs want the same resource—whether it's food, a toy, or even a comfy spot on the sofa—conflict can arise. This happens in domestic dogs and wild dogs alike. But while street dogs tend to focus on mating and food resources, pet dogs often compete for attention, toys, or space.

The problem is, when humans don't understand how dogs communicate, we miss the early warning signs of conflict. This is why enrichment plays such a key role—it reduces frustration, gives dogs appropriate outlets for their natural behaviours, and allows them to think rather than react.

The Changing Brain During Canine Development

A dog's brain isn't a fixed thing—it changes dramatically throughout their life. So I thought it would be cool to have a look at the key stages:

- **In Utero**: Even before they're born, a puppy's brain is being shaped. Maternal stress plays a massive role here—if the mother experiences high levels of stress during pregnancy, the puppies can be born with a heightened sensitivity to stress. This is why selecting a fit, well-fed, and stress-free mother is so important when choosing a puppy.
- **Neonate** (0-2 weeks): At this stage, puppies are completely dependent on their mother. Early-life stress, nutrition, and handling all play a crucial role in shaping how their brain develops.
- **Transitional Period** (2-3 weeks): Eyes and ears open, and the brain starts processing sensory information for the first time. What they see and hear at this stage can shape their future behaviour.
- **Socialisation Period** (3-12/14 weeks): This is the sensitive window where puppies learn what is safe and what is dangerous. Owners often think that they alone shape their dog's personality, but what happened before they got the dog plays a massive role. Miss this stage, and social deficits become much harder to fix.
- **Juvenile Period** (3-6 months): The brain starts pruning unnecessary connections—meaning that the experiences the dog has now will determine what they retain and what they forget.
- **Social Maturity** (12-36 months, depending on breed): This is where the brain undergoes its final major changes. Think of it as the dog's version of the teenage years—if they've been relying on an anxious brain, that's what gets hardwired. If they've been learning to problem-solve calmly, that's what gets strengthened.
- **Adult to Senior** (6+ years): The brain becomes more stable but can start declining. Keeping the brain active through enrichment slows cognitive decline and helps prevent issues like dementia in senior dogs.

Why Enrichment Helps Shape a Healthy Brain

- It strengthens the cortex: The thinking brain (frontal cortex) controls problem-solving and emotional regulation. Enrichment-based activities, like problem-solving for food, literally improve a dog's ability to think and regulate their emotions.
- It prevents stress damage: Chronic stress shrinks parts of the brain (hippocampus) and enlarges the fear-processing centre (amygdala), making dogs more reactive. Enrichment helps dogs recover from stress and build resilience.
- It provides control: Lack of control over stress leads to helplessness. Giving dogs choices—like picking between toys or engaging in scent work—restores a sense of control and reduces anxiety.

As Rick Hanson puts it, *"Your brain is like Velcro for negative experiences but Teflon for positive ones."* Dogs are wired to remember negative experiences more easily than positive ones, which is why we need to outnumber the bad with the good. Every time you engage your dog in enrichment, you're helping strengthen the right connections in their brain, making them more confident, calm, and capable.

So, if you take one thing from this chapter, let it be this: Enrichment isn't just 'fun.' It's shaping your dog's brain, influencing their emotional health, and giving them the best possible chance at a happy, balanced life.

Chapter 3
Understanding Predatory Motor Patterns

Have you ever watched your dog stalk a squirrel, chase after a ball with laser focus, or pounce on a squeaky toy as if their life depended on it? These behaviours may seem like harmless fun (or occasionally embarrassing chaos), but they're actually part of something much deeper: your dog's predatory motor patterns. And trust me, understanding these can be a game-changer for how you live with and train your dog.

Predatory motor patterns (PMP) are a series of instinctual behaviours inherited from your dog's wild ancestors. These behaviours, once essential for survival, are now hardwired into your dog. The sequence is like nature's playlist: orient, eye, stalk, chase, grab-bite, and kill-bite. Depending on the breed and purpose for which they were developed, some of these behaviours are stronger than others. For example, herding dogs like Border Collies excel at the eye and stalk phases, while terriers are all about that grab-bite energy. Retrievers? They love the chase and grab-bite but generally skip the kill-bite part (thank goodness).

Why Understanding PMP Matters

If we don't understand our dog's natural behaviours, we can't effectively meet their needs or prevent unwanted actions. Ignoring these instincts can lead to frustration—for you and your dog. Have you ever wondered why your Labrador keeps stealing socks or why your terrier obsessively digs in the garden? That's their predatory motor pattern trying to play itself out, and they're finding their own ways to fulfil it.

Here's the good news: you can't remove these instincts (and honestly, why would you want to?), but you can channel them in appropriate ways. That's where enrichment comes in. By providing outlets that mimic elements of the predatory sequence, you're not just keeping your dog entertained—you're giving them a sense of fulfilment and reducing the likelihood of behaviours that drive you up the wall.

The PMP Sequence: A Closer Look

I'll break it down step-by-step, because I'm nice like that.

- **Orient:** Your dog's ears prick up, and their head swivels toward a noise, movement, or smell. This is the moment they've locked onto a potential target.
- **Eye:** They fixate. You know the look—that intense, unblinking stare that says, "I'm about to make my move."
- **Stalk:** Slow and steady, they creep forward, calculating every step.
- **Chase:** The fun begins! They're off like a rocket, chasing their quarry with single-minded determination.
- **Grab-Bite:** If they catch it, they'll clamp down. This is often the climax for many dogs, especially retrievers and terriers.
- **Kill-Bite:** Don't worry, most domestic dogs don't get here—unless you count annihilating a squeaky toy as "kill-bite light."

Why Dogs Love PMP Activities

Engaging in these behaviours releases dopamine in your dog's brain. It's like nature's reward system—every step of the sequence makes them feel good. This is why scatter feeding (letting your dog search for kibble rather than plonking it in a bowl) is so effective. The act of sniffing and searching engages their seeking system, giving them a burst of satisfaction.

How Enrichment Channels PMP Safely

Instead of letting these instincts run wild—literally—we can provide structured activities that allow dogs to practice elements of the sequence in a safe and controlled way. Here's some examples to get your enrichment juices flowing:

- **Orient & Eye:** Try scent trails or hide treats around your home or garden. Let your dog use their nose and eyes to find them.
- **Stalk:** Flirt poles are brilliant for this. They mimic prey movement and allow your dog to practice stalking and pouncing.
- **Chase:** Toss a ball or frisbee, but keep it varied. Repetitive chasing can lead to over-arousal, so mix it up with other activities such as having your dog chase after you.
- **Grab-Bite:** Tug-of-war is a great way to fulfil this instinct. Despite myths, playing tug won't make your dog aggressive. Just have clear rules, like a solid "leave it" command.

- **Kill-Bite:** Give them durable toys they can shred or chew. For some dogs, destroying a cardboard box is immensely satisfying—and it's cheaper than replacing your shoes!

Just like us, dogs need activities that engage their minds and bodies in ways that feel natural and rewarding. By understanding their PMP and finding ways to work with it, we're setting them up for happier, healthier lives.

Key Takeaways for Dog Owners

1. **Recognise the Sequence:** Knowing your dog's unique PMP tendencies helps you understand why they do what they do, so in other words, do some research on the breed of dog you have.
2. **Channel, Don't Suppress:** You can't eliminate these instincts, but you can direct them into appropriate activities. Think of it like a computer, when you purchase a computer, it comes with built-in hardware that cannot be erased.
3. **Variety is Vital:** Keep things fresh to avoid over-arousal or fixation on a single activity.
4. **Have Fun Together:** Enrichment isn't just for your dog—it's a chance to bond and create memories.

Remember, enrichment isn't about stopping behaviours; it's about working with your dog's natural instincts to bring out the best in them. So go on, get creative, and let your dog's inner predator thrive—in the most appropriate, controlled way possible. Trust me, giving them the chance to display these behaviours in a controlled environment will prevent a lot of unwanted behaviours outside on walks, saving you those awkward embarrassing moments.

Chapter 4
The Power of Experiences

Every year, I make it a point to take Thursdays and Fridays off during the school holidays to spend quality time with my four kids. It's a great time for adventures, laughs (normally at my expense), and making memories that I wouldn't trade for anything in the world. Funny how life works, isn't it? There was a time I couldn't imagine having kids, and now I can't imagine life without them.

I am all about variety, and every time I am off with the children we aim to do something different. It's all about exploring new places and experiencing new things. One of our standout trips last year was to Eden Camp in Yorkshire. For those of you who might not know (especially if you're on the other side of the pond), Eden Camp is a museum unlike any other. It's set in a former World War II prisoner of war camp and offers an immersive experience that brings history to life.

Walking through the old barracks, surrounded by recreated scenes of wartime Britain, we were transported to another time. The sights, the sounds, the smells—it all worked together to paint a vivid picture of life during the war. For me and the kids, it wasn't just a day out; it was an experience. It sparked conversations about history, resilience, and humanity. It engaged all our senses, made us think, and created lasting memories. Oh, and the ice cream was good too…you can't have a day out without some nutritional enrichment, right?

Places like Eden Camp get me thinking about the concept of enrichment and how vital meaningful experiences are—not just for us humans, but for our dogs too. Just like that day out enriched our lives, the activities we provide for our dogs can offer them the same sense of engagement, joy, and fulfilment.

What Do I Mean by Experiences for Dogs?

When we talk about offering experiences to our dogs, we're not just talking about throwing a ball in the garden or taking them on the same walk every day. While those activities have their place, they're only scratching the surface of what's possible. Experiences, in the context of enrichment, are about variety, stimulation, and opportunities for our dogs to engage their senses, minds, and bodies in meaningful ways.

Think about it like this: if you did the exact same thing every day, ate the same food, walked the same route, and never encountered anything new, how would you feel? Bored, right? Our dogs feel the same way. They crave novelty, exploration, and the chance to use their natural instincts. Offering them diverse experiences is one of the best ways to keep them happy, healthy, and mentally stimulated.

Why Experiences Matter

Dogs are naturally curious, intelligent beings. They're hardwired to sniff, search, solve problems, and explore their environment. Without these outlets, they can become bored, frustrated, and even develop behavioural issues. Enrichment through experiences meets their instinctual needs, providing:

- **Mental Stimulation:** Engaging their brains prevents boredom and keeps them sharp.
- **Physical Activity:** Experiences often involve movement, which helps keep dogs fit and healthy.
- **Social Interaction:** Many experiences offer opportunities for dogs to interact with people and other dogs.
- **Sensory Engagement:** Dogs experience the world through their senses, and new sights, sounds, and smells are incredibly enriching.
- **Confidence Building:** Trying new things and overcoming challenges can boost a dog's confidence and resilience.

Turning Everyday Activities into Enrichment

The beauty of offering experiences is that they don't have to be elaborate or expensive. With a little creativity, even the simplest activities can become enriching. Here are some ideas:

- **Explore New Places:** Take your dog on walks in new locations. A trip to the woods, a quiet beach trip, or even a different part of your neighbourhood can provide a wealth of new smells and sights.

- **Create a Scent Adventure:** Scatter treats in your garden or around your home and let your dog sniff them out. This taps into their natural foraging instincts and provides both mental and sensory stimulation.
- **Set Up a DIY Obstacle Course:** Use household items to create a mini agility course. Chairs to weave through, blankets to crawl under, and low tables to jump over can turn a regular day at home into an exciting adventure.
- **Interactive Toys and Puzzles:** Food-dispensing toys, puzzle feeders, and games that make your dog think are fantastic ways to provide mental stimulation.
- **Play Hide and Seek:** Hide somewhere in your house and call your dog's name. The excitement of finding you is a great reward for them! (I'll add, we do not need to make it too difficult, I don't expect you to barricade yourself in your loft.)

When I first opened the doors to my daycare back in 2015, I knew I wanted to create something different. From day one, my goal was to build an enrichment-based daycare that offered experiences not just for the dogs but also for the humans on the other side of the lead. This wasn't just about keeping dogs busy—it was about creating a place where dogs could thrive and owners could feel like they were part of something special.

Not only do I offer enrichment through my daycare, but I also offer it through The Sandancer Superhero Dog Club, my online training club (only cool dogs and owners allowed). Every month, I set fun and engaging challenges for the owners and their dogs. The best part? They can earn badges for their dogs as they complete these challenges. (Pretty cool if I do say so myself!) It's not just about the badges, though. It's about building stronger bonds, boosting confidence, and giving owners tools to make life with their dogs more enriching and rewarding. That's why I do this— because enrichment isn't just for the dogs. It's for all of us. I've seen first-hand how offering new experiences can transform a dog's life. Take Max, a Labrador I did some one-on-one training with. Max had a habit of getting into mischief—chewing furniture, digging up the garden, you name it, typical adolescent Labrador. His owners were at their wits' end. After chatting with them, we introduced Max to a variety of enrichment activities, including scent work and interactive play. The change was incredible. Max's destructive behaviour decreased, and he became a calmer, happier dog. Small changes with huge results, and that is just one example. I could write a full book on the number of humans I have recommended to do more enrichment activities with their dogs and the changes it has made.

Making Enrichment a Habit

Offering experiences doesn't have to be a once-in-a-while thing. By weaving enrichment into your daily routine, you can give your dog a richer, more fulfilling life. Start small, experiment with different activities, and pay attention to what your dog enjoys the most. Remember, variety is key. The more diverse the experiences, the more engaged and satisfied your dog will be.

When I look back on my trips with the kids, whether it's to Eden Camp, Beamish, or just a simple day exploring somewhere new, I'm reminded of how powerful experiences are and this is seen in the smiling faces from the kids and the fact they go to bed early following an adventure too…always a bonus. They're the moments that stay with us, the stories we tell, and the memories we cherish. Our dogs deserve those moments too. By offering them enriching experiences, we're not just giving them something to do; we're giving them a life filled with joy, curiosity, and connection.

So, what are you waiting for? Plan your next adventure with your dog and see how it transforms both their life and yours. Trust me, you'll never look back.

Chapter 5
Training and Enrichment – The Perfect Partnership

Training and enrichment—two words that might seem separate at first but are actually the ultimate dream team when it comes to raising happy, healthy, and well-behaved dogs. You see, training isn't just about teaching your dog to sit or stay. When done correctly, it's a form of enrichment that engages your dog's mind, strengthens your bond, and taps into their natural instincts. In this chapter, we're going to explore how training can double as enrichment and why it's a game-changer for both you and your furry friend.

But first, let's address a little something I like to call "The Dominance Dilemma."

The Myth of Dominance Training

Ah, the dominance theory. Just saying those words makes me cringe. It's like nails on a chalkboard to anyone who's spent time studying modern, science-based training methods for dogs. Yet, despite being debunked countless times, the dominance theory continues to linger like an unwanted party guest. It's time to give it the boot and I hope after reading this chapter you think to yourself, what a pile of shit that dominance theory is and then you go off and educate your friends, or better yet recommend them to read this book.

The dominance theory—for those of you lucky enough to have avoided it—suggests that dogs are constantly vying for power in your household. According to this outdated notion, your dog's adorable antics are actually cunning attempts to overthrow you as the "alpha" and claim your living room as their kingdom. Sounds ridiculous, doesn't it? Yes my dear friend it does and that's because it is.

Where Did This Nonsense Come From?

Blame the 1930s and 1940s. Swiss animal behaviourist Rudolph Schenkel conducted studies on captive zoo wolves, observing their behaviour in artificial, high-stress conditions. These unrelated wolves, crammed into an enclosure, displayed aggressive and hierarchical behaviours as they competed for resources such as food, mates, resting areas etc. Schenkel concluded that wolves operate on a dominance hierarchy where the "alpha" leads the pack.

Fast forward a few decades, and this idea was applied to domestic dogs because... well, why not? Dogs descended from wolves, so clearly they must be trying to dominate us, right? Wrong. That's like saying we're trying to dominate each other because we share DNA with chimpanzees. It doesn't add up.

The Reality of Wolves (and Dogs)

Modern research, aided by advancements in technology, has revealed that wild wolves don't operate on dominance. Instead, they live as family units. The so-called "alpha" is typically just the parent, guiding the pack with cooperative behaviours to ensure survival. They work together, not against each other.

Dogs, while related to wolves, have evolved alongside humans for thousands of years. Their goal isn't to dominate us; it's to coexist with us. They look to us for guidance, care, and—most importantly—a relationship built on trust, not fear. Why would they want to dominate the humans that literally provide them with everything?

The Problems with Dominance-Based Training

Let's be honest for a moment. Dominance-based training isn't just ineffective; it's downright harmful. Here's why:

1. **It Ruins Trust:** Imagine being punished for trying to communicate your needs. That's what happens when dogs are harshly reprimanded for behaviours that are often rooted in fear or confusion.
2. **It Creates Fear:** Dogs trained under dominance methods live in a state of anxiety, always waiting for the next punishment. Fear-based training doesn't teach; it traumatizes.
3. **It Ignores the Real Issue:** Most so-called "dominant" behaviours are actually normal dog behaviours or stress responses. By focusing on "putting the dog in its place," dominance training fails to address the root cause.

Let me tell you about Bluey, a sweet little spaniel who came to me after a disastrous encounter with a so-called "trainer." This trainer—and I use that term loosely—advised Bluey's owner to use dominance techniques like pinning him to the ground and snatching his food away mid-meal. The result? Bluey became fearful, aggressive, and completely shut down. It took months of positive reinforcement training to rebuild his trust and confidence.

The Shift to Positive Training

Thankfully, we're seeing a shift away from these outdated methods, thanks to amazing trainers like Karen Pryor. Karen revolutionized dog training by introducing modern, science-backed techniques rooted in positive reinforcement. Her work has left behind a legacy that continues to change lives—for both dogs and their humans.

Positive training focuses on rewarding desirable behaviours rather than punishing unwanted ones. It's about setting your dog up for success and building a partnership based on trust, respect, and mutual understanding.

Training as Enrichment

So, how does training tie into enrichment? When done correctly, training engages your dog's brain, taps into their natural instincts, and provides them with a sense of accomplishment. Here's how:

1. **Mental Stimulation:** Teaching new commands or tricks challenges your dog to think and problem-solve.
2. **Physical Exercise:** Many training activities involve movement, which helps burn energy.
3. **Confidence Building:** Learning and succeeding boosts your dog's self-esteem.
4. **Bond Strengthening:** Training is a shared activity that deepens your connection with your dog.

Examples of Enrichment-Based Training

1. Trick Training

Teaching tricks like "spin," "paw," or "roll over" isn't just cute—it's enriching! Tricks engage your dog's mind and provide a fun way for them to earn rewards.

2. Scent Work

Dogs love to use their noses. Hide treats around your home or garden and let your dog sniff them out. This activity satisfies their natural foraging instincts and keeps them mentally engaged.

3. Agility Training

Set up a mini agility course in your garden using household items. Jumping over broomsticks, weaving through chairs, and crawling under tables are all great ways to combine physical and mental stimulation.

4. Name Recognition

Teach your dog to recognise the names of their toys. Ask them to fetch specific ones, turning playtime into a brain workout.

The Importance of Patience and Consistency

Training takes time. It's not an overnight fix; it's a journey. But the rewards? They're worth every second. A well-trained dog isn't just obedient; they're confident, happy, and deeply connected to you.

Remember: your dog isn't trying to dominate you. They're trying to navigate a world that doesn't always make sense to them. Your job is to guide them with kindness and patience, showing them the ropes in a way they can understand.

Moving Forward

If you've used dominance-based methods in the past, don't beat yourself up. As the wise Rafiki once said in *The Lion King*, "It's in the past. It doesn't matter." What matters is what you do from this moment on. Embrace positive, enrichment-based training methods, and watch as your dog thrives in ways you never thought possible.

Let's leave the dominance theory where it belongs—in the past—and focus on building a brighter, kinder future for our dogs. Because at the end of the day, training isn't about controlling your dog; it's about learning and growing together.

Chapter 6
The Five Pillars of Enrichment

When I first stumbled upon the concept of enrichment and truly understood its importance, I had one of those lightbulb moments. You know, the kind where you suddenly realise, "Wait, I've been doing this for years and never realised!" Whether it was building cardboard mazes for my childhood hamster, Hammy, or introducing new experiences to the dogs at daycare, it clicked for me: enrichment is about so much more than just keeping animals busy. It's about meeting their needs, respecting their instincts, and giving them a life that's truly fulfilling.

To keep things organized, we can break enrichment down into five pillars, which we roughly touched upon in a previous chapter: Sensory, Intellectual, Environmental, Social, and Physical. I've come back to the five pillars of enrichment because these pillars work together to create a balanced, enriching life for your dog. So grab a cup of tea, settle in, and let's dive into each one. Trust me, by the end, you'll be buzzing with ideas for your own dog.

1. Sensory Enrichment

Dogs live through their senses. Their noses are roughly 40 times more powerful than ours, their hearing can pick up frequencies we can only dream of, and even their sense of touch plays a crucial role in how they navigate the world. Sensory enrichment is about giving your dog new experiences that engage those incredible senses and keep their brains ticking.

Why It Matters: Sensory enrichment helps dogs stay curious and mentally stimulated. It's particularly useful for reducing anxiety and boredom because it shifts their focus from what's stressing them out to something they can actively explore.

Last year, when I took two daycare dogs on the miniature train ride at the park, I wasn't thinking, "This will be a ground-breaking sensory experience." I just thought, "This will be fun!" But as the train chugged along, I noticed how they perked up at the sound of the train whistle, sniffed the breeze, and scanned the passing scenery. It was like sensory overload (in a good way), and it reminded me just how much dogs benefit from new sights, smells, and sounds.

Examples of Sensory Enrichment:

1. **Sniffari Walks:** Let your dog take the lead on a walk and sniff to their heart's content. Forget the destination—it's all about the journey.
2. **Scent Work at Home:** Hide treats around the house or garden and encourage your dog to sniff them out.
3. **Texture Exploration:** Lay out different surfaces like bubble wrap (don't leave unsupervised please), grass mats, sand, or even crinkly paper for your dog to explore.
4. **Doggy Spa Day:** Incorporate gentle massages, grooming, and dog-safe aromatherapy.
5. **Sound Play:** Play recordings of nature sounds or use a squeaky toy to engage your dog's hearing.

2. Intellectual Enrichment

If sensory enrichment is the appetizer, intellectual enrichment is the main course. This pillar focuses on challenging your dog's brain with problem-solving, learning, and decision-making. Think of it as giving your dog a Sudoku puzzle but with treats.

Why It Matters: Mental stimulation is just as important as physical exercise. A dog who has something to think about is less likely to bark at the postman, chew your sofa, or rearrange your bins. Intellectual enrichment boosts confidence, builds resilience, and prevents boredom-driven mischief.

Back in 2023, I launched my online training club for dogs, The Sandancer Superhero Dog Club. Every month, we have monthly tele classes where I share my pearls of wisdom with the members, we have Q&A sessions, a vault of resources at a finger's click away, and every month I set owners off on a challenge to work on at home with their dog. The aim of these challenges is to encourage the dog to really think and use their brain, which has had some amazing results from our members. Plus, as if that's not all, these members also get to earn badges for their dogs that they can display at home to show off their superhero skills. Be sure to check out the bonus section at the end of the book, as I have included 2 months free access to the club so you can see for yourself just how amazing it is.

Examples of Intellectual Enrichment:

1. **Puzzle Feeders:** Use KONGs, snuffle mats, or treat-dispensing balls to make mealtimes more engaging.
2. **Interactive Toys:** Invest in toys that require your dog to solve a puzzle to get to the reward.
3. **Name the Toy Game:** Teach your dog to fetch specific toys by name.
4. **DIY Cardboard Maze:** Create a maze out of boxes and hide treats at the end.
5. **Shell Game:** Place a treat under one of three cups, shuffle them, and let your dog find the prize.

3. Environmental Enrichment

Environmental enrichment is about making your dog's surroundings more interesting and stimulating. It could mean creating spaces where they can dig, climb, or explore, or just rearranging their environment to keep things fresh.

Why It Matters: Dogs need variety in their environment to prevent boredom and frustration. A dynamic environment encourages them to express natural behaviours like exploring, digging, and climbing.

One of my favourite daycare activities is transforming the Scent Space for our monthly themes. The Scent Space idea came into my head during the dreaded COVID lockdown (Am I allowed to say the C word yet?) when I was sat at home. The daycare had just had a restructure, and my old office was now empty and collecting dust. I thought about a few different ideas such as a little shop or a groomer, but then my love for enrichment took charge, and I decided to create a Room of Requirement for the dogs—more on that later.

Examples of Environmental Enrichment:

1. **Digging Pit:** Fill a sandbox or kiddie pool with sand and bury toys or treats for your dog to dig up.
2. **Obstacle Course:** Use household items like chairs, broomsticks, and cushions to create a fun course.
3. **Rotating Toys:** Keep things fresh by swapping out toys every week.
4. **Climbing Areas:** Create safe spaces where your dog can climb, like ramps or low platforms.

Garden Obstacle Hunt: Hide toys or treats behind plants, under pots, or beneath garden decorations to encourage exploration and problem-solving.

4. Social Enrichment

Dogs are social animals, and social enrichment is about giving them opportunities to interact—whether that's with other dogs, humans, or even other species. I think this is where many owners go wrong; they believe their dog MUST have other canine friends. As much as some dogs love that, others don't. For many dogs, the best friend they want is YOU, and it's important we teach our dogs we are the be-all and end-all. But rest assured, my human friend, if you start offering enrichment to your dog, they are going to have all eyes and ears just for YOU.

Why It Matters: Positive social interactions build confidence and teach dogs how to communicate appropriately. Social enrichment also strengthens the bond between you and your dog.

When I opened my daycare back in 2015, one of my main goals was to create a space where dogs could form friendships. I've seen nervous dogs blossom into social butterflies after spending time in a supportive group environment. Watching them play and communicate with each other is one of the most rewarding parts of my job. I also wanted to create a 'family' and not just be like every other daycare. I wanted to involve owners in the activities we do as much as the dogs, and I think it's safe to say I have done that with our annual Curry nights, annual Christmas premiere nights (that's right, I do a Christmas production featuring the daycare dogs), and I like to get the owners involved in various other activities such as our Easter Bonnet parade, our Santa for Strays, and I can't forget the time there was a murder at daycare, and the owners had to guess which dog killed poor Tim Jackson (don't worry, spoiler alert, I didn't really die).

Examples of Social Enrichment:

1. **Playdates:** Arrange safe meetups with other dogs who share a similar play style.
2. **Interactive Games:** Play games like fetch or tug-of-war with your dog.
3. **Training Together:** Join a group training class to combine learning with socialisation.
4. **"Follow the Leader" Game:** Practice various activities while the dog follows you, like walking, jumping over small obstacles, or moving around furniture.
5. **Hide and Seek:** Hide somewhere in the house (behind a door, in a closet, under a blanket), and the dog has to find you.

5. Physical Enrichment

Last but certainly not least, physical enrichment focuses on keeping your dog's body active. Whether it's through play, exercise, or agility training, this pillar ensures your dog stays fit and healthy.

Why It Matters: Exercise isn't just about burning off energy. It helps maintain a healthy weight, reduces stress, and improves overall wellbeing. Plus, a tired dog is a happy dog!

I enjoy doing karate as my form of physical enrichment, which I have done for a number of years now with my children. It helps keep me fit, happy, reduces stress, and it certainly tires me out... although, at times I do wish I was more flexible... the joys of getting older, I guess.

Examples of Physical Enrichment:

1. **Flirt Pole Fun:** Use a flirt pole with a toy attached for your dog to chase.
2. **Backyard Agility:** Set up hurdles, tunnels, and weave poles in your garden.
3. **Tug-of-War:** A simple game that's great for bonding and strength-building.
4. **Fetch with a Twist:** Add challenges like throwing the ball into a kiddie pool or up a small hill.
5. **Water Play:** Let your dog splash around in a shallow pool or run through a sprinkler.

The Five Pillars of Enrichment—Sensory, Intellectual, Environmental, Social, and Physical—are the foundation of a happy, fulfilled dog. They're not just about keeping your dog occupied; they're about honouring who they are and what they need to thrive.

By incorporating these pillars into your dog's daily life, you'll not only see a happier, healthier dog but also strengthen the bond you share. And isn't that what it's all about? Whether it's a sniffari, a playdate, or a homemade agility course, enrichment is your way of saying, "I see you, I understand you, and I want you to have the best life possible."

Chapter 7
The Importance of Enrichment

Imagine your dog, a highly intelligent and social creature, sitting there staring at you. What do they want? They don't need to check their phone for new notifications, prepare dinner for the kids, or go to work, but they certainly need mental and physical stimulation. When dogs don't get the proper enrichment, when their natural instincts aren't nurtured or challenged, they'll find something to do. And trust me, it won't be what you want them to do.

We've all seen the typical "problem behaviours" that result from a lack of enrichment—chewing furniture, digging up the garden, barking at nothing in particular, or tearing up shoes. But what is truly going on beneath the surface when your dog starts to behave in ways that feel more destructive than constructive?

The Dog's Incredible Brain: An Overlooked Powerhouse

Let's quickly go back to talking about the brain—your dog's brain, to be specific. A dog's brain is actually very similar to a human's in terms of complexity but with a few key differences. Dogs' brains are wired for learning, adaptability, and problem-solving, which is why enrichment is so important. When a dog's brain isn't stimulated in ways that fulfil its needs—such as through exercise, training, or even simple puzzle-solving—they can become bored, frustrated, and even stressed.

The dog's brain weighs around 1/10th of what a human brain does, but don't be fooled by its size. Despite its relatively small size, a dog's brain is designed to process information and solve problems. The dog is not the type to just sit and vegetate (well, not unless they're a Bull dog and then, bless them, they do nap a lot). Left unchecked, the dog's brain seeks stimulation. But without proper outlets, that stimulation can often come in the form of undesirable behaviours.

A Bored Dog Will Find Trouble

You know what happens when dogs don't get enough mental stimulation? They get creative. They become like those kids who, when left to their own devices for too long, start coming up with all sorts of trouble. Think of Kevin from Home Alone and sledging down his stairs! A dog who's bored might chew your shoes, dig up your garden, bark incessantly, or engage in other unwanted behaviours. What they're really doing is seeking out the mental stimulation they need.

One of the most important things to understand is that a dog's need for enrichment isn't just for fun or entertainment—it's crucial for their wellbeing. When we fail to meet that need, their brains become "idle," which often leads to frustration. That frustration manifests itself in behaviour we may consider "bad." But let's face it, your dog isn't being "bad" for the sake of it—they're just trying to find a way to stay mentally active. And unfortunately, sometimes that means your favourite shoes get chewed to bits.

The Science of Enrichment

The science behind enrichment is rooted in the concept of neuroplasticity (I'm sorry, I know that's a big word)—the brain's ability to adapt, change, and reorganize itself. This means that when a dog experiences different stimuli, such as new sights, smells, sounds, and challenges, their brain forms new neural connections. Enrichment promotes the growth of these connections, keeping the brain sharp, active, and healthy.

Research has shown that a lack of enrichment can lead to a host of problems, including anxiety, stress, and even physical health issues. Just like humans, dogs need a good balance of physical and mental activities to stay healthy. If we don't provide opportunities for mental stimulation, it's like putting a child in front of a TV for hours a day—eventually, they'll get bored and start looking for trouble.

Enrichment Through the Ages: The Evolution of a Dog's Needs

Throughout history, dogs were bred to perform specific tasks—herding, hunting, guarding, retrieving, and companionship. The early ancestors of dogs were constantly working to survive and fulfil their role in human society. Over time, domestication changed the nature of these tasks, but the dogs' instincts didn't go away. They still crave work, stimulation, and purpose.

This brings us to today. While our dogs no longer need to hunt or herd for food, they still carry those instincts. In fact, the domesticated dog is now one of the most versatile animals, capable of performing a wide range of roles, from therapy dog to search and rescue worker. But to perform these jobs well, a dog needs to be mentally engaged. If we fail to provide enrichment, we stifle their natural potential and limit their ability to thrive in our homes.

The Negative Power of Unmet Needs

Let's talk about something serious for a moment: the power of negative experiences. Your dog's experiences shape their behaviour and emotional responses. If we continually expose them to situations that are stressful, uncomfortable, or unpleasant (like stressful vet visits, grooming, or long car rides), we are giving them negative memories that stick. Think of it this way: if every time you went to the doctor, you had a bad experience, eventually, you'd associate the doctor's office with stress and anxiety. Or better yet, think about the dentist. I hate the dentist (I mean not the dentist personally, she's very nice, but the experience of going). As a child, I had a lot of work done on my teeth, which involved anaesthesia, needles, pain, the lot. And due to that, I absolutely hate going to the dentist, even just for my routine check-ups.

This is why positive enrichment activities are crucial. If we want our dogs to learn that the world is a safe, fun, and stimulating place, we need to make sure their good experiences with us outnumber the bad ones. This doesn't mean we can avoid all negative experiences (I mean, we all have to get the dog to the vet at some point), but it does mean that we need to balance them with a wealth of positive, enriching experiences.

The "Corny" Tale of York Maze

To illustrate this, let me share a recent experience of mine with my kids. We visited York Maze, and let me tell you—it was an adventure like no other. The theme for the day was corn, and from the moment we arrived, it was clear that no detail had been overlooked. It was, to put it simply, *corn-tastic*

43

(yes, I went there). Every corner of the maze was designed to entertain, from the Cornstruction Zone to the thrilling Cornula one race track, and even a Cobsleigh Run. There was a Volcano to climb (I didn't do so great there, but hey, I tried), and a hilarious water balloon fight in Utter Cornage, where I emerged victorious (because, you know, the kids can't win at everything…I call it life lessons).

We also had fun getting lost in the Giant Corn Maze and testing our skills at Angry Crows, a fun twist on the classic carnival game. By the end of the day, we were covered in foam, dancing alongside costumed corn on the cobs.

Why am I telling you all this? Because this experience was enriching for all of us. It wasn't just about having fun—it was about engaging all of our senses, interacting with new and exciting things, and leaving with positive memories. My kids are already asking if we can go again next year, and I'm sure they'll remember that day for a long time. They had a blast, and their brains were buzzing with new experiences. That's what we want for our dogs too—experiences that engage them, challenge them, and make their lives richer and more enjoyable. And it keeps things positive.

When it comes to your dog's brain, enrichment is not just a luxury or an extra treat to toss into the mix. It's a necessity. Just like we need variety in our lives to feel fulfilled, our dogs need mental stimulation, physical challenges, and positive interactions to thrive.

Without enrichment, your dog's brain will search for ways to stay engaged—often in ways that we don't find desirable. It's our job to ensure that they have plenty of enriching experiences to satisfy their needs. Just like my kids and I had a *corny* blast at York Maze, we can help our dogs experience the world in ways that are fulfilling, positive, and mentally stimulating. So, give your dog the experiences they need to grow and thrive—and watch as their behaviour improves, their bond with you strengthens, and their life becomes as rich as a day spent in a corn maze (with fewer foam parties, though, maybe).

In the end, the more positive experiences you provide, the more likely your dog will learn to interact with the world in a calm, balanced way. And isn't that what we all want for our furry friends? More fun, less frustration.

Chapter 8
Common Myths about Enrichment

Enrichment. It's a word that gets tossed around a lot in the world of dog care, but what does it really mean? How do we, as dog owners, know if we're providing enough mental stimulation, if we're enriching their lives to the fullest? Is it enough to simply hand your dog a snuffle mat or Kong, toss in a treat, and call it a day? As much as I love those toys, they're just scratching the surface of what truly makes a dog's world exciting, fulfilling, and mentally stimulating.

I've worked with a lot of dogs, and time and time again, I see people claiming they've got enrichment all figured out, simply because they've got a few toys in rotation. They often say things like, "Oh, I already use a snuffle mat and a Kong every day." Well, let me tell you, dear reader—there is a world of enrichment opportunities out there that you're missing, and it's time to dive into it deeply.

Is Enrichment Just About Toys?

I can't count how many times I've had clients tell me, "I already do enrichment; I give my dog a snuffle mat and a Kong every day." And while snuffle mats and Kongs are indeed great tools for mental stimulation and enriching a dog's environment, they are far from the only options. Dogs are smart, and just like us, they need variety to keep things interesting. Imagine reading the same book over and over, or watching the same movie over and over, or eating the same meal every day for the rest of your life—eventually, you are going to get bored. It's the same for dogs. (I am not saying we need to be changing our dog's diet, by the way, but we can spice up how we feed it too).

Enrichment doesn't just come from toys and treats—it's about providing new experiences, challenges, and sensory stimulation that tap into your dog's instincts, emotions, and intelligence. Sure, a snuffle mat is a wonderful puzzle feeder, which engages your dog's nose. But what about their sense of sight, hearing, and movement? What about enriching their social skills or giving them more freedom to problem-solve in different ways?

This is where I see a lot of people falling short. They focus too much on the food aspect of enrichment—"Oh, I gave my dog a stuffed Kong" or "I let them sniff through a snuffle mat"—and they overlook the other dimensions of enrichment that can help them thrive. The truth is, enriching a dog's life is more about variety and the right kind of challenge. It's about letting them engage in ways that fulfil their natural instincts.

Is Mental Stimulation Enough; Physical Activity Doesn't Matter or Vice Versa?

I hear this one all the time too: "I give my dog a puzzle toy, so they should be mentally stimulated enough." While mental stimulation is absolutely essential for a dog's wellbeing, it is by no means the whole picture. Dogs, like humans, need both mental and physical exercise to be truly happy and balanced. Without physical activity, mental stimulation can only go so far.

When I work with clients, I often find that they believe a few minutes of puzzle toys are enough to tire their dog out. But here's the thing: dogs are wired to move. Physical activity is just as important for their brains as it is for their muscles. Without enough exercise, a dog can become bored, frustrated, and even anxious. A dog with pent-up energy is much more likely to find trouble—digging, chewing, barking, and other behaviours that we consider problematic.

Physical exercise can complement mental stimulation. Just like humans who enjoy both a good workout and a challenging book, dogs benefit from both. The combination of mental and physical enrichment helps tire them out in a way that leads to relaxation and contentment. And this is why I'm always telling people—mix it up! Play fetch, go for walks, try agility courses, and give them time to explore their environment. Dogs are at their best when both their minds and bodies are engaged. I appreciate that sometimes dogs are unable to get exercise, say, for example, they are on crate rest following surgery, and fear not because there is a chapter later in this book covering that...I'm covering it all in this book.

Is Enrichment a One-Time Deal?

I often encounter people saying that enrichment is a one-time fix. "I gave my dog a new toy last week, and they seemed really excited, so they must be enriched." But enrichment isn't a one-off activity. It's an ongoing process that needs to be continuously integrated into your dog's life. Dogs thrive on novelty, challenge, and change. So, if you're doing the same thing every day and expecting it to keep your dog engaged, you may be setting yourself up for disappointment.

In fact, one of the biggest mistakes people make is assuming that the enrichment they provided last week is enough for the next several weeks. The key to successful enrichment is variety. Dogs love learning new things, and they love being challenged. If you do the same activities over and over, they're not going to feel challenged anymore. And let's face it, if your dog isn't mentally stimulated, they'll likely turn to behaviours you don't want to see.

I remember once working with a dog named Max, a Border Collie with an abundance of energy. His owners were dedicated to providing enrichment, but they had gotten into the habit of giving him the same toys every day. After a while, Max started ignoring them and looking for other things to do—like stealing food off the counter and digging up the backyard. When I encouraged them to change things up and create new challenges for Max, they were amazed at how much more engaged he became. He was like a completely different dog.

Is Enrichment Only for "Problem" Dogs?

Many believe that enrichment is only necessary for dogs with "behaviour problems." People think that as long as their dog is well-behaved, they don't need to worry about enrichment. But the truth is, every dog—regardless of their behaviour—benefits from enrichment. Dogs aren't just pets; they're active, intelligent creatures with needs that go beyond food, water, and a warm bed. Even the calmest, most well-mannered dogs still need mental and physical stimulation to live a fulfilling life.

Take my experience visiting York Maze with my kids. It was a simple family outing, but it was incredibly enriching for everyone. We were engaged in new, exciting activities—things we hadn't experienced before. We had a blast, laughed a lot, and explored every corner of the maze. This is what enrichment can look like for dogs—new experiences, challenges, and opportunities for growth.

So, whether your dog is well-behaved or has a few quirks, enrichment is a tool to help them lead a fuller, more exciting life. Dogs who aren't challenged mentally or physically can still develop behavioural issues, and they may not reach their full potential.

Do All Dogs Like the Same Type of Enrichment?

Here's the thing: just like people, dogs have different preferences, strengths, and personalities. Some dogs love to work on puzzles and sniffing games, while others might prefer running, chasing, or interacting with other dogs. The thought process that all dogs should enjoy the same enrichment activities is one that needs to be debunked.

For instance, I know some dogs who absolutely love their Kongs, while others barely give them a second glance. Some dogs thrive on agility courses, while others prefer a good ol' game of tug-of-war or a simple walk around the neighbourhood. The key to successful enrichment is finding what your dog enjoys and challenging them in ways that suit their personality. More on your dog's personal preferences in the next chapter.

When I work with dogs, I often find that the more you cater to a dog's individual needs, the more effective enrichment becomes. And sometimes, this involves a little trial and error. Try different activities, observe your dog's reactions, and adjust accordingly. Your dog is telling you what they like through their behaviour, and it's up to you to listen.

The bottom line is this: enrichment is not a one-size-fits-all solution. It's a dynamic, ongoing process that requires effort, creativity, and a willingness to explore new possibilities. While snuffle mats, Kongs, and other toys are great starting points, they're just the tip of the iceberg. To truly enrich your dog's life, you need to dive deeper and think outside the box. Be creative, explore new activities, and continuously adapt to meet your dog's ever-evolving needs.

Enrichment is not just about keeping your dog busy—it's about keeping them fulfilled. It's about tapping into their natural instincts, challenging their minds, and giving them opportunities to thrive in a world that is just as exciting as a day spent exploring a corn maze. And just like my kids and I had an unforgettable experience at York Maze, your dog can have a life that's filled with joy, discovery, and plenty of enrichment.

So, don't just settle for the basics. Get out there and give your dog a world of opportunities to grow, learn, and flourish. After all, they're counting on you.

Chapter 9
Understanding What Your Dog Enjoys

Just like people, dogs have their own unique likes, dislikes, and quirks. Some love a good game of fetch, others prefer a sniffari (yes, that's a thing!), while some just want to curl up on the sofa and get belly rubs all day. Understanding what your dog enjoys isn't just about keeping them happy—it's about strengthening your bond, tailoring enrichment activities to their needs, and even improving their training success.

We're All Different—And so Are Dogs

To put it into perspective, let's talk about me for a second (there's a point to it, I promise). If you don't know me already, I'm a bit of a workaholic (okay, maybe a massive workaholic). But when I'm not working, you'll find me doing karate with my kids, Harvey and Darcey. It's something we love doing together—it keeps us active, sharp, and, let's be honest, I love the challenge. If someone took me to a football match, I'd be checking my watch, wondering when I could leave. But take me to a karate competition? I'd be in my element, fully engaged, probably giving a running commentary on every move.

Now, apply that same thinking to your dog. Just because someone tells you that all dogs love chasing a ball doesn't mean your dog will. Some dogs live for fetch, while others look at you like, "You threw it, you go get it." The key is to experiment and find out what truly excites your dog.

Finding Your Dog's Favourite Things

The best way to discover what your dog enjoys is through trial and observation. Here are a few simple tests to help you figure out exactly what your dog loves:

1. Food Preferences

Not all treats are created equal in the eyes (or noses) of a dog. Some dogs will do backflips for cheese, while others will sell their soul for a piece of chicken.

- Try placing a variety of tiny food samples (cheese, chicken, fish, apple, peanut butter, carrot, etc.) in a muffin tin.
- See which ones your dog eats first, second, or ignores completely.
- This is also a great way to find high-value treats for training (especially outdoor training).

2. Toy Preferences

Some dogs love a good game of tug, while others prefer a squeaky toy or a soft plush to cuddle.

- Scatter different toys on the floor and see which one your dog goes for first.
- Repeat this a few times to see if they consistently pick the same one or if their preference changes.
- Use their favourite toy as a reward in training or to motivate them in games.

Buddy's favourite thing is a Croc, not an actual dog toy. Nope, he prefers those hideous Crocs people seem to wear on their feet all the time now. If I have a Croc in my hand, WW3 could be happening behind Buddy and he wouldn't care because that Croc really motivates him.

3. Where They Like to Be Stroked

Just because YOU love giving belly rubs doesn't mean your dog loves receiving them.

- Gently stroke different parts of your dog's body and observe their reaction.
- A relaxed dog will lean into your touch, close their eyes, or even sigh contentedly.
- If they move away, flick their ears, or lick their lips, they're politely telling you, "No thanks." That's your sign to move away.

4. Activities They Love

Beyond the Walk

Your dog's favourite activities can tell you a lot about their personality.

- Do they sniff everything in sight? They might enjoy scent-based games.
- Do they love running and chasing? They might enjoy agility.
- Do they love problem-solving? Puzzle toys and trick training could be their thing.

Dogs Might Surprise You!

I'll be honest—if someone had told me my Whippet, Buddy, would love dancing, I'd have laughed. But during the COVID lockdown, I launched my first online 'Dancing with Dogs' course, and Buddy was right there, bopping along. He absolutely loved it! I never thought a Whippet would be into dancing, but there he was, wagging his tail and showing off his moves. The point? Never assume what your dog will or won't like. Try new things—you might be surprised!

Why Knowing Your Dog's Preferences Matters

So why does all of this matter? Because knowing what your dog enjoys makes everything else easier.

- Training Becomes More Effective : If your dog loves cheese more than dry biscuits, use cheese as a reward and watch their recall skyrocket.
- Recall Improves : If you know your dog's favourite toy or game, you can use it as a reward for coming back to you.
- Enrichment Becomes Meaningful : Enrichment isn't just about throwing random activities at your dog—it's about choosing activities that make them happy and tick those natural desires.

There are approximately 8 billion people (the last time I counted) in the world, each different from one another... yes, even identical twins have their own unique preferences. You may be reading this book and think karate is not for me and that's fine; you may prefer something else, which is equally fine. There are over 900 million dogs in the world, and just like us mere humans, they too have their own unique preferences. So, find what they love, and you'll not only enrich their life but also strengthen your bond in the process.

Chapter 10
Breed-specific Enrichment: Giving Dogs What They Were Born to Do

If you've spent any time around dogs—whether in a daycare setting like mine or just as a dog owner—you've probably noticed something: different breeds have different quirks. Some dogs are relentless fetchers, some are obsessive diggers, some will follow a scent trail for miles, and some will chase anything that moves (including your unsuspecting ankles). These behaviours aren't random; they're hardwired into the dog's DNA. And if we want to keep our dogs happy, fulfilled, and mentally stimulated, we need to work with those instincts, not against them.

Let's dive into why breed-specific enrichment is so important and how we can tailor activities to let dogs do what they were born to do.

Built-In Behaviours: The Motor Patterns and Instinctual Drives

We've touched on motor patterns and instinctual behaviours in a previous chapter, but let's quickly revisit them because they are the foundation of breed-specific enrichment. As a reminder (because if you are like me, you may read a few chapters of a book, put it down, and then come back to it later), motor patterns are the sequence of behaviours a dog is naturally inclined to perform based on what they were historically bred to do. For example, a Border Collie doesn't need to be told to herd—it just does. A Labrador Retriever will instinctively chase, grab, and bring things back. A Beagle will follow a scent trail with such laser focus that you could wave a steak in front of its face, and it wouldn't even blink. These behaviours are embedded deep within them, passed down from their working ancestors.

If we don't provide an outlet for these instincts, dogs will find their own way to express them—often in ways we don't like. A bored herding dog might start herding the kids. A frustrated terrier might dig up your prize-winning flower beds. A scent hound with no scent games might take itself off on an unscheduled 'adventure.'

This is why breed-specific enrichment is crucial. It helps to satisfy their natural drives in a controlled, fun way that benefits both dog and owner. So let's break it down breed by breed.

Terrier-Type Dogs: The Digging, Tunnelling, and Tenacious Trouble-Makers

Terriers are small, sturdy, and built to go to ground. Historically, they were bred to hunt and kill vermin, often tunnelling underground to flush out their prey. No one had to teach them to do this—it's in their blood. And while they might not have to hunt for their dinner anymore, that instinct to dig and burrow hasn't gone anywhere.

If you've got a terrier, you've probably noticed that they love to dig. Some owners try to discourage this, but let's be real—telling a terrier not to dig is like telling me not to eat cake. It's not happening. Instead, we need to direct that energy into appropriate outlets.

Enrichment Ideas for Terriers:

- Dig Pits: Set up a designated digging area in the garden or use a sandbox filled with loose soil, shredded paper, or even ball pit balls.
- Tunnels and Burrowing Games: Use fabric tunnels or blankets draped over chairs to create makeshift burrows for them to wriggle through.
- Scent-Based Challenges: Hide treats or toys underground or in soft surfaces to mimic the experience of unearthing prey.

At daycare, our terriers love a good digging session, and giving them an outlet for their energy means they don't try to 'redecorate' the Scent Space floor!

Scent Hounds: The Super-Sniffers

Scent hounds—like Beagles, Bloodhounds, and Basset Hounds—have an almost supernatural ability to detect scent. Their bodies are literally designed for sniffing: long ears help funnel scent particles towards their noses, and loose facial skin traps the scent around their muzzles. But this amazing ability can sometimes be a nightmare for owners. Once a scent hound picks up a trail, they are GONE. And yelling their name is about as effective as whispering into the wind.

Enrichment Ideas for Scent Hounds:

- Scent Trails: Lay down scent trails using treats or a trail of brine from a tin of tuna to create a fun 'treasure hunt' for your dog.
- Snuffle Mats and Puzzle Feeders: Encourage foraging behaviours by hiding food in different textured mats and games.
- Hide and Seek: Hide their favourite toy or treat around the house and let them track it down.

We've learned at daycare that scent hounds need regular sniffing activities to keep them mentally satisfied. If we don't provide it, they start 'investigating' things we'd rather they didn't.

Herding Dogs: The Brainy Workaholics

Border Collies, Australian Shepherds, and German Shepherds are some of the most intelligent dogs around. They were bred to move livestock, and their ability to anticipate movement, problem-solve, and work with humans is unparalleled.

A Collie doesn't need to be taught to herd—it just does it. It will naturally circle, crouch, and 'eye' its target, whether that's sheep, other dogs, or (unfortunately) your kids. Since most owners don't have access to sheep, we need to find alternative ways to engage their herding instincts.

Enrichment Ideas for Herding Dogs:

- Flirt Poles: These long poles with a toy attached mimic the movement of prey, giving herding dogs a fantastic outlet for their chase instincts.
- Directional Training: Teaching left, right, stop, and go commands can simulate herding work.
- Obstacle Courses: Setting up hurdles, tunnels, and weave poles lets them use their agility and quick thinking.

Sighthounds: The Speed Demons

Sighthounds—like Greyhounds, Whippets, and Salukis—are built for speed. They're designed to chase fast-moving prey over long distances. If you've ever thrown a ball for a Whippet, you'll know they launch after it at full throttle. But if that ball stops moving, they often lose interest.

Enrichment Ideas for Sighthounds:

- Flirt Poles: These are particularly effective for sighthounds, as they mimic fast-moving prey.
- Chase Games: A moving target is key—dragging a toy along the ground can keep them engaged.
- Sprint Training: Set up an open area where they can practice short bursts of speed.

I spent a huge amount of time teaching my whippets to bring things back to me as I do not want them to chase after something, lose interest when it stops, and then refocus on a squirrel or another dog and be one of those owners (you know which ones I mean). So now Buddy and Bea get to enjoy the chase, but they will return the ball because they want me to throw it again for them.

Why Breed-Specific Enrichment Matters

Understanding a dog's breed-specific needs helps in so many ways:

- Training Becomes Easier: If you know what motivates your dog, you can use that to reinforce behaviours. A scent hound will work for sniffing opportunities, while a herding dog thrives on structured tasks.
- Recall Improves: Instead of battling a dog's natural instincts, you can work with them. A sighthound with no outlet for chasing will bolt after anything that moves, but if you give them structured chase games, they're more likely to stay engaged with you.
- It Prevents Behavioural Problems: Frustrated instincts often lead to destructive behaviours. If you don't give a terrier something to dig, they'll dig your sofa.

Going back to the previous chapter, we need to provide activities for our dogs that they enjoy and remember every dog is different. You may have a herding dog, but that doesn't mean they won't enjoy scent work, or you may have a scent hound, and that doesn't mean they won't enjoy some agility or parkour (more on parkour later). A lot of the time, it is about working with the dog you have and getting to know the dog you have.

So, let's embrace who our dogs are. Let's work with their instincts, not against them. And let's make their lives as enriching as possible! I sure hope I am motivating you enough and selling you the benefits of enrichment.

Chapter 11
Enrichment for Anxious, Shy, and Reactive Dogs: Confidence Building with Safety First

As a canine behaviourist, I work with a lot of reactive dogs, shy dogs, and dogs that resource guard. One of the biggest things I emphasize when it comes to offering enrichment (and, honestly, anything else with dogs) is safety. Safety should be the foundation of everything we do—because if we set a dog up in a situation where they feel unsafe, we aren't helping them, we're making things worse. Enrichment is meant to build confidence, reduce anxiety, and bring joy, not cause stress or conflict.

Safety First! (Because No One Wants a Lawsuit)

I don't know about you, but it feels like health and safety has gone to a whole new level over the years. Remember when people used to ride bikes without helmets and slide down metal slides in the summer, burning themselves in the process? Yeah, fun times and those days are gone. Now, we have risk assessments for everything. And you know what? When it comes to dogs, I guess that's a good thing.

When we offer enrichment, we need to do a mental risk assessment first. Before you toss out a snuffle mat, hand over a stuffed Kong, or set up a group play session, ask yourself:

- Will the dog guard this item? If so, maybe a communal food-based activity isn't the best idea.
- Is the dog in a safe environment? If they're reactive, is there enough space? If they're anxious, is it quiet and calm?
- Am I in a safe position? If a dog gets overstimulated or protective, am I in a good spot to step away if needed?

This kind of mental risk assessment should become second nature. The goal is to enrich the dog's life, not create a situation that leads to stress, fights, or worse—an injury.

Why Enrichment is a Game-Changer for Anxious Dogs

Anxiety in dogs can show up in different ways—some shut down and hide, while others bark, lunge, or pace. The beauty of enrichment is that it gives these dogs an outlet. It gives them something positive to focus on, something they can control. And that is huge and let's not forget the more positive experiences to outnumber the negative ones, the better.

Think about how you feel when you're anxious. If someone threw you into a loud, overwhelming room full of strangers and told you to "just relax," would that work? No. But if you had a small, comfortable space where you could do something you love, like read a book, play a game, or listen to music, you'd start to feel better. Dogs are the same.

Some great enrichment ideas for anxious dogs include:

- Scent work : Encourages natural behaviours in a low-pressure way.
- Shredding boxes : Gives them a satisfying way to release tension. Please note though don't allow them to eat the box, and if there is a risk of guarding then that's a big no against your risk assessment straight away.
- Lick mats : The repetitive licking can have a soothing effect.
- Puzzle feeders : Keeps their brain engaged while giving them a sense of control.
- Calming music or scent diffusers : Sets the mood and helps bring their stress levels down.

The key is to introduce things gradually and never force a dog into an enrichment activity. They need to explore it at their own pace.

Enrichment for Shy Dogs: Bringing Out the Inner Rockstar

Shy dogs often need a little extra help coming out of their shell, and the right enrichment can work wonders. But just like with anxious dogs, it's all about setting them up for success.

The biggest mistake people make with shy dogs is throwing them straight into overwhelming situations. Picture this: a dog who's unsure of new environments gets placed into a bustling daycare group with ten boisterous Labradors. That's like tossing an introvert into a nightclub and expecting them to have the time of their life. Not happening. That is why we are very careful and selective with the dogs we take at daycare and why every dog needs an assessment. Any signs of the dog being unhappy and the assessment ends. It's as simple as that.

Instead, build confidence in smaller steps:

- One-on-one play : Let them engage with a calm, friendly dog first.
- Desensitization activities : Expose them slowly to new things in a controlled way.
- Interactive games with their handler : Tug, fetch, or gentle training sessions to build trust.
- Obstacle courses : Things like small tunnels or ramps can help build confidence.

The goal is to empower the dog, not push them too far too fast. Each small win builds their confidence.

Enrichment for Reactive Dogs: Giving an Outlet for All That Energy

Reactivity isn't just "bad behaviour"—it's often a dog's way of expressing stress, frustration, or over-arousal. The best way to manage it? Give them an appropriate outlet. Reactive dogs need structured, engaging activities that help them release energy in a positive way rather than reacting to triggers.

Some fantastic enrichment ideas include:

- Flirt poles : Let them chase and engage their prey drive in a controlled way.
- Scent trails : Helps redirect focus and encourages problem-solving.
- Structured tug sessions : Can be a great way to channel excitement while reinforcing rules.
- Fetch (in a controlled setting !): Some reactive dogs thrive with a game of fetch in a secure environment.
- Calm-focused training games : Teaching things like "find it" or "place" helps build impulse control.

Again, the mental risk assessment comes into play. Know the dog, know their triggers, and set them up for success.

Resource Guarders: Setting Them Up for Success

Resource guarding is a natural behaviour, but if not managed properly, it can become dangerous. Some dogs guard food, others guard toys, and some even guard people. The golden rule? Don't set them up to fail. If you know a dog guards certain things, don't put them in a situation where they feel the need to protect it.

Some tips:

- Use enrichment that doesn't trigger guarding : Scatter feeding works well because the food isn't in one big pile.
- Give them space : Let them enjoy their enrichment in a quiet, separate area.
- Avoid high-value items in group settings : If a dog is prone to guarding, don't hand out stuffed Kongs in a room full of other dogs.
- Teach trading games : Reinforce that giving something up leads to something better.

With resource guarders, respect is key. They aren't being "dominant" or "bad"—they're just trying to protect something they find valuable. Our job is to help them feel safe so they don't feel the need to guard.

Making Sure Enrichment Works for Every Dog

At daycare, we tailor enrichment to each individual. It's also why we run a boot camp for new dogs. We don't just throw them into the deep end; we take the time to understand what they enjoy, what makes them comfortable, and what helps them thrive.

I've seen too many "bog-standard" daycares that treat all dogs the same. That's not how it should be. Dogs are individuals. They deserve enrichment that suits them, makes them happy, and helps them be their best selves.

So, next time you plan an enrichment activity, do a mental risk assessment, think about the dog in front of you, and remember: The goal is to build confidence, not stress!

Chapter 12
The Room of Requirement: A Dog's Version

If you're a Harry Potter fan (and let's be honest, if you're not, I question your life choices), then you'll know all about the Room of Requirement. For those who have somehow managed to avoid the world of wizardry, let me give you a quick rundown. The Room of Requirement is this magical, ever-changing space in Hogwarts that appears only when a witch or wizard truly needs it. You could be wandering the castle halls, thinking, "I really need a place to hide this contraband," and BAM! The room appears, filled with secret passageways and towering stacks of forgotten junk. Or if you're part of Dumbledore's Army and need a hidden training ground, it transforms into a fully equipped combat dojo. The room senses the needs of the individual and provides exactly what they require at that moment in time.

Now, you might be thinking, "Great, but what does this have to do with dogs?" Well, let me introduce you to the canine version of the Room of Requirement: The Scent Space at my daycare.

The Birth of the Scent Space: The Ultimate Dog Room of Requirement

When I first opened my daycare back in 2014, I had a vision. I didn't want to run a bog-standard daycare where dogs just ran around all day like caffeinated toddlers at a soft play centre. No, I wanted to create a daycare that gave dogs what they actually needed—not just what people assumed they needed. Dogs need structure, mental stimulation, and rest just as much as they need physical exercise. And one of the most overlooked needs? Their incredible ability to sniff and engage their brains.

That's where the Scent Space came in. I created a dedicated area at daycare where dogs could come and use their noses, get one-on-one time, and experience the joy of problem-solving. It became our own Room of Requirement, offering enrichment, confidence building, and a sense of purpose for the dogs in our care. And you know what? They LOVED it.

We use it for scent trails, puzzle-solving, calming activities, and more. Every month, we slap on a fresh coat of paint and create a new themed experience for the dogs. Variety is key! One month it's a jungle adventure, the next it's a pirate treasure hunt—it's like Disneyland, but for dogs.

And here's the kicker—what started as a unique idea in my daycare has now spread worldwide! Through my additional business, Enrich University, which I run with my business partner Dom, we teach other daycare owners how to incorporate scent spaces and enrichment-based activities into their own facilities. And let me tell you, the daycare owners we work with? They are absolutely smashing it. Seeing scent spaces pop up in daycares across the world, all starting from a little idea that sparked in my brain, makes me incredibly proud and yes, I'm going to blow my own trumpet!

Do You Need to Build a Scent Space at Home?

Now, I don't expect you to read this and think, "Crikey, I need to build an entire scent space in my house." That would be excessive (though, if you do, I'd love to see pictures). However, what I *would love* is for you to start providing more enrichment activities for your dog.

Every month, as part of my Sandancer Superhero Dog Club, I run monthly challenges to encourage owners to engage their dogs in new and exciting ways. We'll talk about these more in another chapter, but the key takeaway here is that dogs thrive on variety. They love using their brains, and it's our job to give them opportunities to do so.

From Vet Nurse to Enrichment Evangelist

When I hung up my vet nurse scrubs for the last time in 2014, I knew I wanted to do something different. I wanted to create an enrichment-based daycare that actually *benefited* the dogs, rather than just serving as a holding pen for hyperactive fur missiles.

And I'll be honest here—when I first opened, I had a bit of a shock. The cost of running a daycare was astronomical. Utility bills, fuel prices, staff wages—none of this was covered in the 'dream big' part of my business plan. So, I couldn't offer the planned enrichment programs I do now straight away. But you live and learn. Now, I make sure every single month has a fresh theme, a new experience, and a balanced structure of physical exercise, mental stimulation, and rest time.

Why? Because dogs need balance. Letting them run riot all day isn't good for them. They need structure. They need guidance. And most of all, they need enrichment.

Lessons from PT Barnum: Be the Greatest Showman for Your Dog

Now, let's talk about my *other* obsession—The Greatest Showman. When it first came out, I refused to get in on the hype (much like my initial resistance to Harry Potter—don't ask, I have issues). But when I finally watched it? I was hooked. And the more I learned about PT Barnum, the more I admired his approach to entertainment.

When he started out, there were already loads of travelling circuses around. But what made him different was that he *thought outside the box* . He had elephants walking the streets. Clowns visiting sick children in hospitals. When his circus was in town, you *knew* about it. He made it an *experience.*

That's what I want to do with my daycare. I don't want to be just another daycare—I want to be the daycare that changes the game. The one that actually gives dogs what they need, rather than what people think they need. And if you take anything from this book, let it be this:

Just because most dog owners don't offer enrichment doesn't mean *you* shouldn't.

Dogs Deserve Choices

We get dogs as part of our families, but we often forget one crucial thing: every decision in their lives is made by us. When they eat, when they walk, where they sleep, what toys they get—it's all dictated by us. Imagine living a life where you had zero choices. It wouldn't be much fun, would it?

This is why enrichment is so important. It gives dogs opportunities to think, make choices, and engage with the world in a way that satisfies their natural instincts. It builds confidence, reduces anxiety, and improves overall wellbeing.

In the world of science, Jaak Panksepp identified seven primary emotional systems that drive behaviour in animals and humans alike:

1. Seeking
2. Fear
3. Rage
4. Lust
5. Care
6. Panic/Grief
7. Play

Dogs, just like us, experience emotions. Their behaviour is deeply tied to their emotional states, which is why offering them a life filled with enrichment is crucial for their emotional wellbeing.

So, something else to take from this chapter: your dog deserves more than the bog-standard approach. Whether it's creating a scent trail in your garden, setting up a puzzle game, or just giving them choices in their daily routine—find ways to enrich their lives.

And if you ever doubt whether it's worth the effort, just remember—when dogs engage in enrichment, they're not just having fun. They're fulfilling their emotional and mental needs. And that, my friend, is the real magic the best dog owner can provide.

Chapter 13
Sniffing Out New Adventures: From the Big Apple to the Canine Nose

I have always wanted to go to America. It was one of those places I'd dreamed of visiting, but between running an enrichment-based daycare, having four children and being up to my eyeballs in snuffle mats, sand pits, and themed activities for dogs, I hadn't quite made it across the pond. That all changed in 2024 when I finally got my chance—I was heading to Hershey, Pennsylvania, to launch Enrich University at a daycare expo. But before I got there, I had one amazing night in New York City, and let me tell you, my mind was absolutely blown.

If you've ever been to NYC, you'll understand what I mean. If you haven't, imagine stepping into a film set where everything is twice the size you expect it to be, the streets are alive at all hours, and you genuinely feel like you might get run over at any given moment. I had barely blinked, and there I was, smack bang in the middle of the city I had wanted to see all my life. And let's get one thing straight—I only got a tiny snippet of it, but I already know I need to go back. Central Park, in particular, is high on my list. A huge green oasis in the middle of the madness? That's my kind of place.

Now, I wasn't just wandering the streets aimlessly. I also had the chance to see *Back to the Future: The Musical* on Broadway. And wow. Bringing a classic film like *Back to the Future* to the stage is a bold move, but they absolutely smashed it. The moment that iconic theme tune hit, I had goosebumps. Trust me when I say it was an experience I will never forget.

Speaking of experiences, let's talk about Hershey. Yes, *that* Hershey, the place where they make the chocolate. Let me tell you, Hershey takes its chocolate identity *very* seriously. The streetlights are shaped like Hershey's Kisses. There's a Chocolate Avenue. My hotel room even had chocolate-scented shampoo, which is a fantastic novelty... unless, like me, you don't have any hair. But hey, it's the thought that counts.

And this brings me back to an important point: experiences matter. We touched on this a few times in previous chapters, but this trip really hammered it home for me. New experiences keep life exciting. They challenge us, broaden our horizons, and make us crave even more. As I sit writing this chapter, I already have another trip planned, this time to Las Vegas for another dog daycare ad pet boarding expo. You'd better believe I'll be soaking up every second of that one, too.

But here's the thing—humans aren't the only ones who thrive on new experiences. Dogs do, too. And while I had my mind blown by the sheer scale of NYC and the fact that *Hershey has chocolate-scented toiletries*, dogs experience the world in an entirely different way. You see, we have our eyes. Dogs? They have their noses. And this is where we get to the juicy part of this chapter: scent.

If I could sum up what I want you to take from this chapter in one sentence, it would be this: Stop dragging your dog away from sniffs and start embracing their superpower.

Now, before we get into the juicy details of how scent work can transform your relationship with your dog, let's talk about perspective. As I've said, humans, we "see" the world. The more we see, the safer we feel. We scope out a room when we walk in. We scan faces in a crowd. If we can see it, we can process it.

Dogs? They smell the world. They sniff first, then hear, then (if necessary) look. It's a completely different way of experiencing life. And yet, we constantly try to force them into *our* way of doing things. We rush them on walks, pull them away from fascinating scents, and expect them to focus when their brains are screaming, *THERE'S A STORY WRITTEN IN URINE HERE AND I NEED TO READ IT.*

So, let's shift our thinking and start seeing the world from a dog's nose-first perspective.

The Science of Sniffing – Your Dog's Superpower

If you've ever had a dog embarrass you by shoving their nose somewhere it absolutely shouldn't be, you've probably already figured out that scent is important to them. But what you might not know is *just how much* scent dominates their world.

Beyond the Walk

Here are some fun facts for you:

Dogs have around 220 million scent receptors, compared to our measly 5 million. That's a pretty huge difference. The part of a dog's brain that processes scent is 40 times larger than ours, taking into account relative sizes. They don't just smell things – they decode entire stories from a single sniff. A lamppost to us is just a lamppost. A lamppost to a dog is a social networking hub full of messages left by other dogs. They know who was there, when they were there, and possibly even what mood they were in when they passed by.

Their noses are so powerful that they can detect certain illnesses, locate missing persons, and even tell the difference between identical twins based on scent alone. But that's not all. Jacobson's organ (also called the vomeronasal organ) allows dogs to pick up pheromones, meaning they can literally smell emotions. Yes, your dog knows when you're stressed before you do.

And here's something that really blew my mind when I first learned about it: sniffing actually releases dopamine in a dog's brain. The SEEKING system (discovered by Jaak Panksepp, legend) is activated through scent work, giving dogs a dopamine hit and making them feel happy and fulfilled. This means that just allowing a dog to sniff more can make them calmer, more focused, and more content overall.

Why Scent Work is a Game-Changer for Your Dog

Now, you might be thinking, *Okay, cool, dogs like sniffing. What's that got to do with me?*

Well, let me tell you—integrating scent work into your dog's daily routine can solve a lot of common problems.

1. It Calms Anxious Dogs

Dogs who suffer from anxiety can benefit massively from scent work. When a dog engages in sniffing, their heart rate lowers, and their stress levels decrease. Think about the last time you were stressed—maybe you listened to some calming music, went for a walk, or did something that occupied your brain enough to settle your nerves. For dogs, sniffing is that activity. It's self-soothing, it's rewarding, and it helps them feel more secure in their environment.

2. It Boosts Confidence in Shy Dogs

Shy dogs can struggle in new environments, but scent work gives them a job to do. It allows them to explore at their own pace, without overwhelming them with direct interactions. A nervous dog who gets to follow a scent trail builds confidence because they're engaging with their environment in a natural and rewarding way. They're problem-solving, they're achieving success, and they're learning that the world isn't so scary after all.

3. It Helps Reactive Dogs Focus

Reactive dogs often struggle to disengage from triggers. Whether it's another dog, a bike, or a loud noise, once they're locked in, it can be hard to redirect their focus. This is where scent work comes in. When a dog is engaged in sniffing, their brain is fully occupied. It gives them an alternative focus that isn't the thing they usually react to. A dog can't be sniffing intently *and* losing their mind over a passing jogger at the same time. If you can introduce scent-based redirection on walks, you'll find that your dog becomes far more manageable.

4. It Gives High-Energy Dogs an Outlet

Some dogs have boundless energy. You could walk them for hours, and they'd still be bouncing off the walls. But what if I told you that mental stimulation is just as tiring as physical exercise? A dog who spends ten minutes working out a scent puzzle can be *just as tired* as a dog who's been running for an hour. When you tap into your dog's natural SEEKING system, they're engaged in a way that truly satisfies their needs. Less frantic zoomies, more settled contentment.

5. It Strengthens Your Bond

Engaging in scent work with your dog isn't just about keeping them entertained—it's about working together. When you set up a scent trail or a find-the-treat game, you're creating an opportunity for teamwork. Your dog starts to look to you for guidance, they learn to trust you more, and your relationship deepens. You become a source of enrichment, not just a food dispenser or a walk provider.

How to Incorporate Scent Work into Daily Life

You don't need fancy equipment or a dedicated scent space to start making the most of your dog's nose. Here are some easy ways to add scent-based enrichment into your dog's routine:

Scent Postcards

Ever noticed how your dog sniffs you when you come home? That's because they're reading a *scent postcard*. You've been places, met people, and stepped in God-knows-what, and your dog is gathering *all* that information through their nose.

Want to make their life even more exciting? Bring home new scents on purpose. Pick up leaves, twigs, or items from different places and let your dog investigate them.

Scatter Feeding & Hide and Seek Games

Ditch the food bowl and scatter your dog's meals around the garden. Hide treats around the house and let them find them. Use puzzle toys and snuffle mats for feeding. These are such simple changes but make a world of difference to your dog's wellbeing.

Sniffy Walks (aka Let the Dog Do What They Want for Once)

Instead of power-walking your dog like you're on a mission, let them take the lead. Slow down. Let them sniff. Give them choices. Trust me, they'll thank you for it.

When it comes to sniffing just remember, a bird was born to fly. A fish was born to swim. A dog? A dog was born to sniff.

So, let them sniff. It's the easiest, most natural, and most rewarding thing you can do to improve their wellbeing. Fancy doing some scent work with your dog? In the next chapter I've laid out a very simple step-by-step guide on how you can get your dog to find a scented toy hidden around the house or the garden.

Chapter 14
An Introduction to Scent Work

Let's get one thing straight: your dog's nose is an absolute marvel of nature, and it's about time we started treating it like the superpower it is.

We've covered a lot about scent work already in this book, but now it's time to properly introduce it. This chapter is all about breaking down what scent work actually is, why it's so beneficial, and how you can start incorporating it into your dog's life in a structured, engaging, and downright fun way.

What is Scent Work?

Scent work is exactly what it sounds like—teaching your dog to use their nose to find a particular scent. But don't let the simplicity fool you; this is one of the most rewarding activities you can do with your dog.

Scent work is often associated with professional detection dogs—think police K9s sniffing out drugs or missing people. But here's the thing: all dogs have the ability to do scent work, and they absolutely love it. It doesn't matter if you have a working-line Malinois or a couch-potato Cavapoo; their nose is still the strongest tool they have.

And the best part? Scent work is low-impact, highly engaging, and incredibly tiring for your dog.

Let me put it into perspective:

- When a dog is lying down relaxed next to you, their respiration rate is about 15 breaths per minute.
- When they're out on a standard walk, it goes up to around 30 breaths per minute.
- If they're off-lead sprinting around, it jumps to 60 breaths per minute.
- But when a dog is doing high-frequency sniffing? Their respiration rate can reach between 130-200 breaths per minute.

That means that sniffing is an incredibly physical activity. And yet, it's one of the most underutilized forms of enrichment for pet dogs.

So if you're looking for a way to tire your dog out, give them mental stimulation, and strengthen your bond, scent work is the answer.

Why Should You Do Scent Work?

Now that we've established what scent work is, let's talk about why you should be doing it.

1. Your Dog is the Leader

One of the best things about scent work is that it flips the script. Instead of constantly directing your dog, you have to trust them.

In scent work, your dog is in charge. You aren't leading them—they're leading you. Your job is to observe, learn their cues, and celebrate when they make a find. This helps build trust between you and your dog.

2. You Can Do It Anywhere

Unlike agility, which requires a lot of space and equipment, or herding, which—let's be honest—requires sheep, scent work can be done anywhere.

- Your house? Yep.
- The garden? Absolutely.
- A quiet corner of a park? Perfect.
- Inside a car? Why not?

Scent work is one of the most versatile activities because it doesn't require a massive setup. All you need is a scent and a way to hide it.

3. It Builds Confidence

Dogs who are shy, anxious, or reactive can massively benefit from scent work. When a dog is engaged in sniffing, it gives them a job to do, a purpose, and something to focus on.

Ever noticed that your dog seems much calmer after a good sniffing session? That's because sniffing releases dopamine, the happy hormone, making them feel more relaxed and fulfilled.

4. It's Fun and Addictive

Once you get started, I guarantee you'll be hooked. Watching your dog engage their natural instincts is absolutely fascinating. Plus, it's an amazing bonding experience—you'll find yourself completely immersed in the game alongside them.

5. It Helps Introduce Dogs to New Environments

If your dog gets nervous in new places, introducing scent work can help. Giving them a job to do takes their mind off their worries. Instead of stressing about the unfamiliar surroundings, they get to focus on finding the scent. This makes them feel safer and more confident in new places.

Understanding Your Dog's Nose

To really appreciate scent work, you need to understand just how insanely powerful your dog's nose is.

- A dog's sense of smell is between 10,000 to 100,000 times better than a human's.
- Dogs inhale through their nostrils and exhale through the side slits in their nose. This allows them to keep a continuous flow of air and scent going at the same time.
- They can move each nostril independently. That means they can actually tell which direction a scent is coming from.
- When they breathe in, the airflow splits into two paths—one for breathing and one for smelling. That's how they can process scents while still getting oxygen.

In short? Your dog's nose is an absolute masterpiece, and the kindest thing you can do is let them use it.

Getting Started with Scent Work

So now that you're sold on the idea (I'm trusting that you are, anyway), let's talk about how to actually get started.

What You Need

You don't need fancy equipment to start scent work, but here are some things that can help:

- A scent: Start with something simple like catnip, dried oregano, thyme, or basil.
- A small toy: A ball, a DIY tug toy, or anything that can hold scent.
- A clear glass jar or even an empty Tupperware box: To store the scent and infuse it into the toy.
- Some treats: Because motivation is key, and just like we celebrate wins with champagne, dogs can celebrate their wins with some yummy treats.

How to Make Your Own Scent Kit

1. Take around 30g of your chosen scent and place it inside a pocket of kitchen roll.
2. Put the scent and a toy inside a sealed jar.
3. Leave it for 24-72 hours to let the scent transfer.

Starting the Game

1. Start in a quiet room with no distractions.
2. Take the scented toy out and engage your dog in play with it.
3. Once they're loving the game, ask them to "leave" and trade for a treat.
4. Put the toy away—we want them to crave the game.
5. Repeat this for a few days to build excitement. The dog will start to associate the smell of the toy with a fun game with their human.

Building the Search

1. Start in one room playing with your dog and the scented toy. When the dog gets excited with the game, gently hold them (if they are

      happy for you to do that, of course) and throw the scented toy so your dog sees it land in another room.

2. Encourage them to "go find" and celebrate when they get it.
3. Once they're confident and you have practised this a number of times, you can now hide the scented toy behind objects. I find cushions on the floor are a great starting point (unless your dog likes to eat the cushions, of course). Repeat the above exercise where you get the dog excited, but this time, when you throw the toy into the other room, there will be cushions on the floor and your job is to aim to throw the toy to land behind one of those cushions. Tell the dog to "go find" and be ready to celebrate when they do.
4. Increase difficulty by taking them out of the room and hiding the toy without them seeing.
5. Keep increasing the challenge while making it fun! Hide the toy behind cardboard boxes, alongside the sofa, etc. Providing you have spent some time with the beginning stages and you have been consistent with the "go find" command and the celebrations, it won't take long before you are hiding it in all sorts of weird places to try and outsmart your dog. Don't worry, your dog will win every time.
6. Remember to always celebrate the wins, i.e., when the dog finds it.

I have included a free webinar regarding an introduction to scent work in the bonus section of this book to explain this fun activity in more detail.

Once again, if there's one thing I want you to take from this chapter, it's this: let your dog sniff.

It's good for them. It makes them happy. And honestly? It's one of the best ways to bond with them.

So grab a scent, hide a toy, and let the sniffing games begin!

Chapter 15
Building a Bond Through Enrichment

In the last chapter, I discussed celebrating the wins, so I thought this would be a good chapter to follow because, as humans, we are sadly pretty good at reinforcing the unwanted behaviours in our dogs.

Why Bonding Through Enrichment Matters

When we talk about enrichment, we often focus on things like reducing anxiety, building confidence, and preventing boredom. And yes, those things are *massively* important. But what about the relationship it builds between you and your dog? That's what I want to focus on in this chapter.

Dogs are only with us for a fraction of our lives, but to them, *we* are their whole life. Their entire world revolves around what we do, when we do it, and how we interact with them. And yet, as humans, we have this natural phenomenon where we focus on the *bad* behaviours while completely ignoring the good ones.

Think about it—when was the last time you actually *noticed* your dog being calm and well-behaved? Chances are, you didn't. Because when they're just lying down nicely, not causing a fuss, they slip under the radar. But the *second* they bark at the window, jump up at the counter, or steal a sock? Oh, *now* they have your attention.

And here's the problem: whatever gets reinforced gets repeated.

The Kibble Pot: Reinforcing the Right Behaviours

So here's what I want you to do: weigh out your dog's food each morning and take 50 pieces of kibble from their daily allowance. These pieces go into what I like to call *The Pot of Value*. And you're going to use them *exclusively* to reward the behaviours you want repeated.

Let's say your dog is lying in their bed, being calm. Reward.

They hear the doorbell but stay quiet. Reward.

They disengage from barking at the window? Reward.

By consistently rewarding the behaviours you like, your dog will start repeating them because they work! And the best part? You don't have to nag, scream, or get frustrated. You're simply reinforcing what you want more of and ignoring what you don't.

Now, let's talk about that dog that plonks his paw on your lap when you're visiting a friend's house. You know the one. He comes over, sits next to you, and slaps that paw down like you owe him something. And what do most people do? They laugh, say, "Awww, aren't you cute?" and give him a fuss. And guess what? The dog has just learned that this gets him attention.

So, what does he do the next time he wants attention? Plonk .

Dogs are smart. If something gets them what they want, they will absolutely do it again. So instead of reinforcing behaviours accidentally, let's do it intentionally.

Frustration in Training (And Why Wine Helps)

Now, I know what you're thinking: *But what if my dog just doesn't get it?*

Here's the thing—if your dog isn't succeeding, it's probably because we're not communicating clearly enough. It's not their fault if they don't understand. It's *ours*.

And this is where human frustration kicks in. It's so easy to feel annoyed when training doesn't go to plan. But if you feel yourself getting frustrated, walk away. Count to five. Take some deep breaths. Have a bath. Drink some wine. Do what you need to do to reset yourself, and then go back when you're calmer.

And most importantly, always end a session on a *positive*. If your dog is struggling with something new, finish with something you *know* they can do and reward them for it. Training should be enjoyable for both of you, not a battle of wills.

The Importance of Rest

I remember when I was younger, I *thought* I could party all night long. But as I got older, reality hit—I needed my bed. And your dog, no matter how young or energetic, needs theirs too.

Many owners think that more enrichment = better, but too much stimulation can actually be overwhelming.

Little and often is the key. Some gentle sniffing games, a bit of training, a nice long sniffy walk, and then? *Rest.*

And don't underestimate the bonding power of *just being together.* Some of the best enrichment you can provide is as simple as cuddling on the sofa and watching TV. Dogs don't need to be on the go 24/7. They need downtime, they need relaxation, and they need you.

Dogs don't care about money, fancy houses, or designer clothes. They care about *us.* They care about how we make them feel, how much time we spend with them, and whether we provide them with the love, security, and enrichment they need to thrive.

Let's reward the behaviours we want. Let's be patient when things don't go to plan. Let's embrace rest just as much as activity.

Because at the end of the day, the bond you build with your dog is what truly matters.

Now go grab that kibble pot and get started!

Chapter 16
Mr Miyagi and Food Foraging Enrichment

One morning last year on our way to school, my kids and I stumbled upon a hedgehog wandering around near a busy main road. Now, this wasn't just any hedgehog—this little guy looked *completely* out of sorts, confused, and clearly not in his natural habitat. There were off-lead dogs in the area, a group of curious kids heading towards him, and the ever-present danger of cars zooming by. My old vet nurse instincts kicked in, and I knew I couldn't just leave him there.

So, I did what any normal, sane person would do: I scooped him up, carried him home, and named him Mr. Miyagi. Because, of course, we are *true* Karate Kid fans.

Once home, a quick check-up revealed he was dehydrated, sluggish, and in need of some TLC. I gave him subcutaneous fluids and antibiotics to help with any potential infections and made sure to warm him up because hedgehogs can become *very* lethargic when they're cold. Over the next few days, we saw a massive improvement. He became more active, feistier (let me tell you, I pooped myself every time he hissed at me—I thought hedgehogs were supposed to be all cute and innocent, not this one)—and most importantly, he started eating again.

Now, here's where enrichment came into play. I wanted to help him regain his natural foraging instincts, so I decided to use a snuffle mat to hide some slugs—his absolute *favourite* food. Watching him eagerly sniff out and find the hidden slugs was incredible for both me and the kids. And more importantly, it was essential for *him*. Hedgehogs rely heavily on their sense of smell to find food, and by hiding slugs in the snuffle mat, I was encouraging him to engage in *natural* behaviour.

A few days later, we released Mr. Miyagi back into the wild, where he belonged, healthier, stronger, and ready to take on the world.

So, what does this have to do with dog enrichment? Everything. Just like good old Mr Miyagi, dogs too enjoy foraging for their food.

Have you ever wondered what kind of puzzle solver your dog is? Is he a brain teaser novice, an intermediate thinker, or an absolute puzzle-solving genius? The good news is, with this test, you're about to find out. And the best part? No matter where your dog starts, he can always improve. Enrichment should never cause frustration—our goal is to set them up for success, keep their brains engaged, and make sure they get maximum enjoyment from the process, just like Mr. Miyagi searching for his slugs.

Now, before you panic, failing this test is impossible. There are no wrong answers. The only thing this test does is help you figure out your dog's current level so that you can tailor enrichment games accordingly. Too hard, and your dog might get frustrated and give up. Too easy, and he'll get bored and think you've lost the plot.

The Puzzle Solver Test

To carry out this test, you'll need a few simple household items. Grab a bucket, a toilet roll tube, and a food treat that your dog absolutely loves but won't lose his mind over. You want excitement, not sheer chaos. Place the bucket upside down on the floor next to you and make sure your dog is watching. Take the treat and show it to your dog, letting them sniff and get a real sense of its presence. Then, in full view of your dog, hide the treat under the bucket. Once it's safely hidden, encourage your dog to retrieve it and observe what happens next.

This is where things get interesting. Every dog will respond differently, and how your dog tackles the problem will tell you a lot about their problem-solving skills. Some dogs will look at the bucket, sigh dramatically, and then stare at you as if to say, "This isn't my job, human." Others will bulldoze the bucket, flipping it over in sheer determination. Some will paw, nose, and try different tactics, using their brains to work out the solution.

What Kind of Puzzle Solver is Your Dog?

Some dogs are natural problem solvers, while others need a bit more encouragement. The way your dog reacts to this challenge will put them into one of three categories: beginner, intermediate, or expert.

A beginner-level problem solver is a dog who is predominantly passive. They may briefly sniff at the bucket but will quickly lose interest when they realise they can't immediately get the treat. This type of dog lacks persistence when faced with a challenge and will either look at you for help or wander off entirely, deciding that whatever you're playing at simply isn't worth their time. If this sounds like your dog, don't worry—it just means they need a confidence boost. The best way to help a beginner is to make the game easier. Instead of using the bucket, swap it for a toilet roll tube with the treat inside. This gives them a much higher chance of success and prevents them from getting frustrated.

If your dog is at the intermediate level, they'll give the challenge a solid attempt. They'll paw at the bucket, nudge it, maybe even try to lift it, but if success doesn't come quickly, they may start losing interest. These dogs have problem-solving skills but might need encouragement to keep going. To help them, you can modify the challenge slightly by tilting the bucket so that the treat is partially visible. This small adjustment makes a huge difference, as it reassures the dog that success is possible, motivating them to keep trying.

Finally, we have the expert problem solvers. These dogs are relentless. They don't give up, no matter how tricky the challenge is. They'll use their nose, paws, teeth, and anything else they have at their disposal to figure out how to get the treat. They might knock the bucket over, push it along the floor, or even try lifting it with their teeth. Small failures don't faze them, and they thrive on the challenge. If this sounds like your dog, congratulations—you have a puzzle-solving expert on your hands! You'll need to keep upping the difficulty to keep them engaged, as they'll get bored quickly if the challenge isn't tough enough.

How to Progress Your Dog's Puzzle Skills

Regardless of where your dog starts, every dog can improve. The key is to always make sure they feel successful and that they're enjoying the process. If something is too hard, they'll give up. If it's too easy, they can easily get bored. Finding the sweet spot where they're challenged but still capable of succeeding is the goal.

Dogs, much like humans, enjoy the process of searching more than actually finding. The seeking system in their brain releases dopamine, making the hunt itself incredibly rewarding. This means that as long as there's the possibility of success, your dog will remain engaged. However, if they never succeed, they'll lose interest. Imagine playing a game where you never win—at some point, you'd stop playing, right? The same applies to dogs.

Making Mealtime Enriching

One of the easiest ways to introduce problem-solving into your dog's life is through mealtime enrichment. Instead of just dumping food into a bowl, make your dog work for it in fun and engaging ways. This doesn't mean feeding extra calories—it simply means making their existing meals more exciting.

A great beginner-friendly activity is simply scattering your dog's kibble around the garden or house so they have to sniff it out. This taps into their natural foraging instincts and makes mealtime last longer. If you want to step it up a notch, you can roll kibble inside a towel, stack plastic cups with food hidden between them, or hide treats inside toilet roll tubes. Another fun method is to place food inside a muffin tin and cover the holes with balls, requiring your dog to remove the balls to get to the food.

For intermediate dogs, you can introduce slightly more complex feeding puzzles. One fun idea is lining up your shoes (empty, of course—unless you want a slobbery mess) and placing treats between them. Shoes carry all sorts of interesting scents, making this a multi-sensory experience. You can also use snuffle mats, food-dispensing toys, or even homemade treasure hunts where they have to find their meal hidden around the house.

For the expert-level puzzle solvers, the sky's the limit. You can place treats inside a plastic bottle with holes cut into it, requiring your dog to shake the food out. You can create biscuit drawers that they have to pull open using their teeth. You can even introduce shop-bought puzzle toys that require multiple steps to unlock the reward. The trick with advanced puzzle dogs is to keep them engaged with ever-evolving challenges.

Balancing Enrichment with Rest

Beyond the Walk

While enrichment is fantastic, it's important to strike a balance. More is not always better. I have mentioned this previously, but I shall, for the sake of importance, say again: just like us, dogs need rest, downtime, and relaxation. If you've ever pulled an all-nighter working on something, you'll know that your brain eventually hits a wall. Dogs are the same. Too much mental stimulation without adequate rest can actually lead to stress.

Make sure that after a fun puzzle session, your dog has time to unwind. This can be as simple as curling up on the sofa together, giving them gentle strokes, or just letting them have a nap in a quiet spot. Rest is just as vital to a healthy, happy dog as enrichment is.

Every dog has the ability to become a problem-solving pro. Whether your dog is currently at the beginner stage or already a puzzle master, the key is to meet them where they are and support them in climbing the enrichment ladder. Celebrate their successes, keep things fun, and always remember that it's not about *finding* the food—it's about *enjoying the journey* to get there. Before we move on to the next chapter, I thought I would share a short step-by-step guide on how you can create your own snuffle mat (I'm nice like that).

How to Make Your Own Snuffle Mat

A snuffle mat is a fantastic way to provide enrichment for your dog. It mimics the natural foraging behaviour of sniffing through grass and encourages mental stimulation. Plus, it's easy to make at home!

Materials Needed:

- A rubber mat with holes (like a sink mat or shower mat)
- Fleece fabric (choose multiple colours for a fun look!)
- Scissors

Instructions:

1. Cut the Fleece: Take your fleece fabric and cut it into strips about 1 inch wide and 6-8 inches long.
2. Tie the Strips: Thread each strip through a hole in the rubber mat and tie it in a firm knot. Repeat this process, filling in every hole until the mat is completely covered in fleece strips.

3. Fluff It Up: Once all the fleece strips are tied on, give the mat a good shake to fluff up the fabric and create hiding spots for treats.
4. Introduce It to Your Dog: Scatter some of your dog's food or treats into the mat and let them use their nose to forage for their reward!

A snuffle mat is a great way to engage your dog's natural instincts, slow down fast eaters, and provide mental stimulation all at once. Plus, it's machine washable, so cleanup is easy.

Chapter 17
Non-Food Based Enrichment – Because Not Everything is About Snacks!

It never fails to amaze me how many times I hear, *"My dog isn't motivated by food."* Now, before I roll my eyes too hard and risk injury, let's just break this down for a second. If your dog eats, then they are motivated by food. Period. It's a survival instinct! But I get it—some dogs don't get wildly excited about treats, and that's okay. Maybe your dog is the type to take a biscuit from your hand ever so gently and then politely drop it on the floor as if to say, *"Thanks, but no thanks."* Or maybe they've been free-fed all their life, with food always available, so there's no urgency to earn it. Or maybe there's just no excitement in getting the food, i.e., it's in the corner of the kitchen in a bowl where it has always been. Yawn.

But here's the thing—enrichment is not just about food. Sure, food puzzles and treat games are great, but there is a whole world of non-food-based enrichment that can engage your dog's brain, build confidence, and strengthen your bond in ways that don't involve stuffing their face. So, if you've got a dog that isn't that interested in snacks, fear not—we've got plenty of other options to keep them entertained!

The Power of Play – Games That Don't Require Treats

Games are an excellent way to provide mental and physical stimulation, and they don't require food to be effective. A well-placed game at the right moment can take a relatively joyless task (like a boring, straight-line walk around the block) and turn it into a fun learning experience.

The Shadow Game

This one is simple but brilliant for reinforcing engagement. Start walking in any direction. As soon as your dog catches up with you, mark the moment (a happy "yes!" or clap will do) and keep going. You don't need food to reward this—just movement and engagement. Your dog will start learning to keep an eye on you, making them naturally more responsive.

Hide and Seek

Want to supercharge your recall in a fun way? On your walk, find a spot to hide behind a tree or a bush when your dog isn't looking. The second they start looking for you and find you? Celebrate like you just won the lottery. Your dog will quickly learn that staying connected with you is a fun and rewarding experience in itself. Plus, it taps into their natural seeking and problem-solving instincts.

The Two Ball Game

Perfect for dogs who love fetch but struggle with the concept of *bringing the ball back* . You'll need two identical balls. Throw the first one. When your dog chases it, show them the second ball and make it exciting. The second they drop the first ball, throw the second one in the opposite direction. No more standing in the park yelling, *"Bring it here!"* while your dog prances around smugly with their prize.

Target Training

Teaching your dog to touch a specific object with their nose or paw (like your hand or a target stick) is not only mentally stimulating but also builds engagement. Plus, it can be useful for all sorts of things—guiding your dog into position, teaching tricks, or even as a recall cue in a busy environment.

The Counting Game

This is a brilliant way to build engagement. Okay, we use treats with this one, but it's such a simple, yet amazing exercise, I cannot not share it. Let your dog wander a little, then crouch down and start counting out loud while placing one treat per number. Keep going until your dog notices and starts running toward you. The second they get to you, get up, move to another area, and repeat. The goal is to create anticipation and responsiveness.

High-Energy Fun – Enrichment for Dogs Who Love to Move

Some dogs don't just want to think; they want to move. If you've got a dog who loves physical play, these non-food enrichment activities will give them the workout they crave while keeping their brain engaged.

Flirt Pole Fun

A flirt pole is essentially a giant cat toy for dogs. It consists of a long pole with a rope and a lure attached. You move the lure around in unpredictable ways, and your dog gets to chase it. It's fantastic for engaging prey drive, working on impulse control, and burning off energy in a short amount of time. Plus, it doesn't involve food—just the thrill of the chase!

Parkour for Dogs

Dog parkour, also known as urban agility, is basically the canine version of an adventure playground, and let me tell you—dogs absolutely love it. It's all about using the environment around you as an interactive obstacle course. Instead of just strolling down the street, you turn everyday objects into fun, confidence-boosting challenges. Got a sturdy log? That's a balance beam. A park bench? Perfect for jumping over or weaving under. Low walls? Great for practising precision jumps or controlled step-ups. Even simple things like tree stumps, bike racks, or staircases can be turned into a parkour playground for your dog.

The beauty of parkour is that it builds confidence like nothing else. It teaches dogs to navigate the world in a whole new way, engaging both their body and their brain. A nervous dog might hesitate before stepping up onto a new surface, but with a bit of encouragement, they learn that they *can* do it—making them braver in other areas of life, too. For high-energy dogs, parkour is an amazing way to burn off mental and physicalenergy without needing loads of space. It forces them to think about their movements, improving coordination, body awareness, and overall control.

And the best part? It makes every single walk an adventure. No more "same old, same old" routes where your dog sniffs the same lampposts and pees in the same spots. Instead, you get to explore your surroundings in a whole new way, turning a boring walk into an exciting mission. Whether your dog is leaping onto a boulder like a mountain goat or confidently stepping up onto a tree stump like they own the place, parkour transforms your daily outings into a fun, interactive bonding experience. Plus, let's be honest—it's pretty cool to watch your dog strut their stuff like a little urban explorer!

Find It! (Scent Work for the Win)

We've already covered scent work in a previous chapter, but just to reiterate—this is one of the best non-food enrichment activities out there. Hide a toy or an object with a particular scent and let your dog find it. This engages their natural sniffing instincts and provides fantastic mental stimulation.

Extreme Fetch

Okay, it's still fetch, but with a twist. Change up the rules—throw the ball uphill, into tall grass, or have them find it in a pile of leaves. Adding an extra challenge makes it more rewarding.

Bubbles for Dogs

Yes, bubbles. Some dogs love chasing and popping bubbles, and you can even buy dog-safe bubbles that smell like peanut butter or bacon (if you *do* want a food element involved). This is a great game for dogs who love movement but need a lower-impact activity.

Round Robin Recall

If you have multiple people around, stand in different spots and take turns calling your dog. Each time they come, give them praise and excitement before the next person calls them. This game builds engagement, strengthens recall, and gets the dog moving while making training fun.

Chase Me!

Dogs love movement-based reinforcement. Call your dog excitedly, and as soon as they start running toward you, turn and run the opposite way. The thrill of the chase becomes the reward.

Sniffari Adventures

Instead of rushing through a walk, let your dog dictate the pace and follow their nose. Let them sniff as much as they want. A 20-minute sniffari can be more mentally exhausting than a long jog.

Funder (Fun + Under = FUNDER!)

Funder is all about encouraging your dog to go *under* things. Get them to crawl under tables, squeeze through small gaps, or move under obstacles. It builds confidence and body awareness while engaging their problem-solving skills. You can even have them weaving in and through your legs.

Enrichment is More Than Just Food

While food-based enrichment is great, it's not the *only* way to engage your dog's brain and body. Whether your dog loves to run, chase, sniff, jump, or simply interact with you, there's an activity out there for them. Games, training, and physical challenges all count as enrichment—and sometimes, the most rewarding thing for a dog is simply spending time with their human, engaged in something fun.

So if your dog isn't food-motivated, don't panic. There are countless other ways to keep them happy, engaged, and fulfilled. Now go grab a flirt pole, challenge them to a game of chase, or start your next epic round of hide and seek. Just be prepared—once they realise how much fun non-food enrichment can be, they'll be the ones dragging *you* out to play!

Chapter 18
Making Walks as Enriching as Possible – Because a Boring Walk is an Unhappy Walk

I love where I live. Having the beach on my doorstep means my dogs get to run on the sand, splash in the sea (well, get their paws wet if they feel brave enough), and experience a sensory paradise every time we go. But here's the thing—I don't just take my dogs to the beach. As much as they love it, I know they'd get bored if that was all they ever did. Just like us, dogs need variety. Imagine if you went on the exact same walk every single day, passed the same landmarks, smelled the same smells, and saw the same people. It wouldn't take long before you started to crave something new. Dogs are no different. They might not complain about the monotony the way we would, but that doesn't mean they aren't affected by it.

This is why I'm always looking for new places to take my dogs—woodland trails, urban streets, nature reserves, empty carparks, garden centres, quiet industrial estates—anywhere that provides them with new experiences. Because that's what a walk should be: an experience, not just a form of exercise. Walking the same route every day is like reading the same chapter of a book over and over again. It might have been interesting the first time, but eventually, the excitement wears off. Dogs, just like us, thrive on new adventures, new smells, and new environments.

One of the best ways to make walks more engaging is by introducing the rucksack walk, an idea created by dog trainer Steve Mann. This isn't just about heading out with your dog; it's about turning the walk into a full-blown activity session that engages both their brain and their body. It's about shifting from the mindset of "getting the walk done" to actually enjoying the process together.

A rucksack walk is exactly what it sounds like—you take a small backpack filled with interesting items and use them to make the walk more interactive. The beauty of this is that you don't need any fancy equipment. Before you head out, grab a rucksack and throw in a few items that your dog enjoys—a favourite toy, a ball, maybe even an old towel or a cardboard box. The idea

91

is to use these items at different points during the walk to mix things up and create opportunities for engagement.

Instead of just walking in a straight line, stop at a quiet spot and pull out a toy for a quick game of tug. Hide the toy behind a tree and encourage your dog to find it. Lay down the towel and ask them to interact with it—maybe they have to step on it before they get to move on, or perhaps you shake it around like some kind of wild beast that needs to be 'caught.' The key is interaction—rather than simply marching forward, you're creating moments of play, exploration, and problem-solving.

One of my favourite things to do on a rucksack walk is to introduce random objects for my dogs to investigate. Something as simple as an empty plastic bottle or a pile of leaves can suddenly become an exciting new experience. I might place the object on the ground and encourage my dog to check it out, paw at it, or push it around with their nose. It's all about engagement—keeping their brain ticking while they move through the environment.

Another great feature of a rucksack walk is that it encourages free thinking. Rather than directing your dog's every move, you're giving them the opportunity to engage with their surroundings in their own way. Maybe they choose to interact with the object you've placed in front of them, or maybe they'd rather sniff around the base of a tree. The point is, they're making decisions and problem-solving, rather than just following along on autopilot.

The best part? This kind of walk is physically and mentally fulfilling. Have you ever noticed how dogs seem more tired after a mentally stimulating session than they do after a long physical run? That's because mental work is hard work. A dog who has had to think, explore, and solve problems will come home far more satisfied than one who has just plodded along a pavement for an hour. And let's be honest—it's a lot more fun for us too!

If you've never tried a rucksack walk before, I highly recommend giving it a go. It's one of the easiest ways to make your walks more enriching, and once you start, you'll never look at a standard walk the same way again. Plus, if you're anything like me, you'll enjoy coming up with new and ridiculous ideas for what to put in your rucksack next. Who knew an old dishcloth could be the highlight of a dog's day? One of Buddy's favourite things I add is an old Croc (yes, I'm talking about those ridiculous things people put on their feet); he goes absolutely mad for it.

At the end of the day, walking your dog should be about more than just getting steps in. It should be about connection, engagement, and giving them the chance to experience the world in a way that excites them. So next time you clip on the lead, think about how you can turn your walk into an adventure. Whether it's through a rucksack walk, a new location, or simply letting them stop and sniff more, the goal is to make the walk as fulfilling as possible—for both of you.

Chapter 19
DIY Enrichment on a Budget – Recycle the Recycling

One of the biggest myths about dog enrichment is that it has to be expensive. You see fancy puzzle toys online, all promising to turn your dog into some kind of genius, and you think, *Do I need to take out a second mortgage just to keep my dog entertained?* The answer, my friends, is absolutely not. Enrichment does not need to cost a fortune. In fact, some of the best brain games I've ever created have come from stuff I was about to throw away.

Now, I talk a lot about something called recycling the recycling—a simple but absolute game-changer of a concept. Before I throw anything into the recycling bin, I stop and ask myself, *Could I make a brain game out of this?* And, apart from a few obvious safety hazards like tin cans (because let's be honest, I'd rather not turn enrichment into an episode of 'How to Give Your Dog a Trip to the Vet'), the answer is almost always yes.

So, let's talk about how you can turn everyday household items into free enrichment toys that will keep your dog's brain buzzing and their tail wagging—without spending a single penny.

The Toilet Roll Tube Treasure Hunt

If you have a dog and you don't have a stash of empty toilet roll tubes sitting in a cupboard somewhere, are you even a real dog owner? These things are gold for DIY enrichment. One of the simplest games you can make is a Toilet Roll Tube Treasure Hunt.

Take a handful of empty tubes, place a treat or some kibble inside one (or a few), and then fold the ends down. Mix them up and scatter them across the floor. Your dog has to figure out which tube holds the prize and then work out how to open it. Some will shake it, some will squash it, and some might chew the tube up to release the treats.

If your dog finds this too easy, up the ante! Hide the tubes inside a cardboard box or bury them in a pile of scrunched-up newspaper so they have to sniff out the hidden goodies.

The Cardboard Box Destruction Derby

I don't know about your dogs, but mine love to rip things up. Now, instead of sacrificing a brand-new toy to their destructive tendencies, why not let them go wild on something that was destined for the bin anyway?

Find a cardboard box (we all shop on Amazon, right?) and place some kibble or a favourite toy inside. Seal the edges up loosely so your dog has to figure out how to open it. Some will nudge at the edges, others will rip straight through like a chainsaw. Either way, it's great for their brain, their confidence, and their natural instincts.

The Laundry Basket Lucky Dip

You know those plastic laundry baskets with holes in the sides? Turns out, they're not just for pretending you're going to tackle the mountain of washing. They also make excellent dog enrichment toys.

Turn the basket upside down and place a few treats underneath. Your dog has to figure out how to paw, nudge, or shove the basket to get the treats out. If that's too easy, use heavier objects inside (small toys, balled-up socks) to create extra obstacles.

If you have a small dog, try poking treats through the holes in the sides of the basket so they have to use their nose and paws to fish them out. You can even thread material through the holes such as old tea towels to make it a bit trickier.

The Plastic Bottle Puzzle

You know those expensive treat-dispensing balls you see online? Yeah, you don't need one of those. All you need is an empty plastic bottle.

Take the label off, remove the cap (so they don't swallow it), and pop a few bits of kibble inside. Your dog has to figure out how to bat, roll, and shake the bottle to get the food out. To make it a bit easier, poke a few holes in the sides so the kibble comes out when it's tipped at the right angle.

Want to make it harder? Stuff a few strips of fabric inside the bottle so the treats don't just fall straight out—your dog has to work for it!

Why DIY Enrichment is So Important

People often assume that dogs need fancy, expensive toys to be entertained, but the truth is, they don't. Dogs don't care about price tags—they care about experiences. The best enrichment is about engagement, problem-solving, and variety, and you can create all of that with the stuff lying around your house.

When you start recycling the recycling, you'll see opportunities for enrichment everywhere. That empty egg carton? Perfect for hiding kibble in. That old cereal box? Great for stuffing with treats and scrunched-up newspaper. Even something as simple as a rolled-up towel can become a brain game with a bit of creativity.

The best part? It costs nothing. So next time you go to throw something away, stop and think—could this become a game for your dog? The answer is probably yes. And if you ever feel guilty about the sheer amount of Amazon boxes cluttering your house, just tell yourself you're saving them *for the dog* . Sounds much better than admitting you have an online shopping problem, right?

Chapter 20
The Future of Enrichment – Sticking to the Routine and Measuring Success

So, you've made it this far. You've learned about sniffari walks, DIY enrichment, how to recycle your recycling, and why giving your dog mental stimulation is just as important as giving them physical exercise. But what happens now? You've got all this knowledge—how do you make sure it sticks? The answer is simple: consistency.

Enrichment isn't just a one-off event, a special treat for a rainy Sunday when you feel like being a good dog owner. It's a lifestyle. It's a new way of life for your dog. And like any new routine, the more consistent you are, the more natural it becomes. I always tell people—stick with it, build it into your daily habits, and record the changes you see in your dog.

I don't need you to start a diary and lock it away under your bed like a teenage love journal. But what I do want you to do is pay attention to how enrichment is changing your dog. Are they calmer? Are they demanding less attention from you at inconvenient times? Are they settling quicker in the evening? Do they just seem happier in themselves?

We often think of success in terms of numbers, but when it comes to enrichment, success is measured in behaviour. If your dog is engaging with their activities, if they are more relaxed in the house, if they seem generally more fulfilled—that is your measurement of success. And remember this— if your dog enjoys an activity, even if they've done it a hundred times, do it again. Dogs don't get bored of things they love. Just because your dog is a pro at a game doesn't mean they don't still find joy in it. If anything, mastering a game often makes it more fun.

Finding Time for Enrichment

Now, I know what you're thinking. "But I'm busy!" And trust me, I get it. We all have a million things on our plates. But answer me this:

- How often do you make time to go out with your friends?

- How long do you spend soaking in the bath?
- How long do you sit watching TV?
- How much time do you lounge in bed scrolling through your phone?
- How many times a day do you check your notifications?

I'm not saying you need to stop doing these things. I'm not here to ruin your bath-time relaxation or take away your Netflix marathons. My point is, you make time for the things you enjoy, and yet so many people say they have no time in the day. What if, instead of scrolling through TikTok for 20 minutes, you spent 10 of those minutes setting up an enrichment activity for your dog? What if, instead of sitting down with your morning coffee and scrolling through emails, you took your dog into the garden for a five-minute sniffari? What if, instead of watching the same old episode of *Friends* for the 100 th time, you did a five-minute training session?

The point is, there is time. You just have to choose to use it differently.

And if you really, really struggle with time? Then let's talk about the next best thing—enrichment-based daycare.

Why All Daycares Should Be Offering Enrichment

Now, this is something I feel very strongly about. There are a lot of daycares out there where dogs are just left to run around all day long, burning off physical energy but getting zero mental stimulation. And you know what that leads to? Overtired, overstimulated, stressed-out dogs.

A good daycare doesn't just let dogs run riot. A good daycare structures the day, providing a balance of mental enrichment, physical exercise, and rest. And that's exactly what we do at my daycare.

When dogs come to us, they don't just get plonked in a big open space and left to their own devices. They get one-on-one enrichment activities, tailored to their individual needs. We make sure every dog gets the chance to use their brain, to work on problem-solving skills, to engage in scent work, to enjoy social interactions in a controlled and beneficial way. And, most importantly, they get time to rest. Because just like humans, dogs need downtime to process what they've learned and experienced.

98

The Sandancer Superhero Dog Club – Bringing Enrichment to You

But what if daycare isn't an option? Maybe you work from home. Maybe your dog isn't suited to daycare. Maybe you just want to be more involved in your dog's enrichment yourself. That's where my online club comes in.

The Sandancer Superhero Dog Club is my online training and enrichment community, designed to help you give your dog the very best life possible—no matter how busy you are.

Inside the club, you'll find:

- Monthly challenges to keep things fresh and engaging, and you can even earn badges and a nice little display to showcase your dog's progress—think of it like boys/girls scouts but for dogs.
- A vault of resources including training videos, online courses, and free downloads.
- Training tips and activities that actually work in real-life situations through our monthly live tele classes.
- A community of like-minded dog owners who are on the same journey as you.

And as a thank you for purchasing this book, you'll find a bonus section offering a free trial of the club. That way, you can dive straight in and see the benefits for yourself.

And don't take my word for it. One of my first-ever members of the online club, Jill Everrett kindly said the following:

"I began working with Tim back in lockdown. He had put a free course on to support dogs and their owners. I think the first course was a trick a day for a week. I began working with my beagle, Alfie, every day, 3 to 5 times a day, for short bursts, and I could not believe what Alfie and I achieved together. Alfie had always been a daddy's dog, and I have to say Alfie is now our dog! Our relationship improved significantly with Tim's fabulous courses. I even taught Alfie to dance, with Tim's help!

So when we got the chance to join Tim's Sandancer Superhero Dog Club, it was a must. The webinars that he does are really helpful. The members of the club are really supportive and helpful too. We feel we are better owners because of Tim.

Alfie is now 11 years old, and when he was ten we decided to get a beagle puppy. Quincey arrived, and he was instantly thrown into the monthly challenges that we do with Alfie.

Quincey is an amazing dog, and we believe this is due to all the enrichment he is given on a daily basis. We are always giving him brain games and training him to do the monthly challenges.

Because of Tim, Alfie now listens to us, most of the time. He has been taught to watch us, and because he knows we call him to play a fun game and have food, he is always keeping his eye on us. Alfie was bitten a lot when young by another dog and is unfortunately now a reactive dog. However, through games and loads of praise, he is learning to be less reactive to other dogs. Quincey is learning from Alfie all the time.

We think Tim is a wonderful, caring guy who just wants to help owners and make dogs' lives better. We are very grateful to Tim and the fab online Sandancer Superhero Dog Club!"

This is followed by one of my elite daycare members, Kate Henderson, who is the proud owner of Bronte and her newest addition, Basil:

"Being in The Sandancer Superhero Dog Club has been invaluable to me. We have a 3-year-old border terrier called Bronte who started with frustration reactivity when she was about 1 & 1/2 years old. Alongside some specific 1-2-1 training, the club has provided me with a wealth of additional information and training in both the online vault and monthly teleclasses that has really helped me to understand Bronte and to improve my relationship with her, which in turn has helped massively with managing and dealing with her reactivity.

The monthly challenges are brilliant, as again, they help to build a really strong relationship with your dog as well as provide them with both training and enrichment. I have found that doing the challenges has had a really positive and calming effect on Bronte's general behaviour, as she is working her brain and using all of her senses during training and scent work, both of which really help to tire her out and keep her calm and settled. Her focus and engagement with me have also massively improved too.

The challenges are always fun to do, and the support from the other members is amazing. We all, at some point, have struggled with a particular challenge, and we always make an effort to encourage each other as much as possible and give our own tips on what has worked for us. It's a real community for like-minded dog owners, and it's the best club to be in!

As well as Bronte, we also have a 7-month-old border terrier puppy called Basil, and knowing how beneficial the club has been to me with Bronte, I started taking part in the monthly challenges with him very early on alongside his general puppy training, and the benefits of doing so have been huge. They've helped me to build a solid relationship with him based on fun and trust, and I would honestly say that doing the challenges with him has helped us to avoid pretty much all of the normal naughty puppy behaviours because he is getting really good enrichment and working his brain, which helps to use up his excess puppy energy and results in him being much more calm and less likely to get involved in destructive or naughty behaviours. Definitely a win-win!"

And one of my platinum daycare members, Rod Gutteridge, who is the proud owner of Bertie, says:

"Our border terrier Bertie joined the Pets2impress Daycare Club just over 12 months ago and he has come on leaps and bounds since then. Daycare offers a multitude of fantastic activities, training, 1-1 scent space time, school trips, adventures, and scent adventures. Bertie partakes in all of these. Bertie loves his time at Pets2impress and has made lots of doggie friends. The staff are all professional, very knowledgeable, and caring towards the dogs in their care.

Bertie is also a proud member of The Sandancer Superhero Dog Club and every month he participates in challenges that we do at home with him, which Bertie embraces. Once the challenges are complete, badges are issued and collected.

We had 1-1 training with Tim and this was a massive success for both myself and Bertie—yes, humans need training too!"

Believe it if you will, but I didn't even have to pay these guys to say that, they just love being part of the club. When I first launched the club, I was extremely busy with behaviour appointments and 1-1 training, and I felt I did not have enough time to be able to help all that needed my help. One of my aims in life is to help as many owners and dogs as I can, so I decided to launch the online club and I have never looked back. It's a free invitation to join, and I know I speak for the other members when I say you will be made to feel very welcome.

The Future of Enrichment – Where Do We Go From Here?

If you've made it this far in the book, you already understand the power of enrichment. You've learned how it can build confidence, reduce anxiety, prevent problem behaviours, and strengthen the bond between you and your dog. The question now is, what's next?

The future of enrichment isn't just about giving dogs things to do—it's about changing the way we think about their needs. It's about making enrichment the norm, not the exception. It's about moving away from the old-school idea that a "well-exercised dog" just needs a long walk and instead recognising that mental exercise is just as important as physical exercise.

It's also about education. More and more dog owners are realising the importance of enrichment, but there's still work to be done. Daycares, trainers, vets, and dog professionals need to spread the message that enrichment is a key part of a dog's wellbeing—not just an optional extra.

And most importantly, it's about commitment. If you've learned one thing from this book, I hope it's that enrichment isn't a one-time thing. It's something that should become part of your dog's daily life, just like food, water, and exercise.

In the UK, the RSPCA (Royal Society for the Prevention of Cruelty to Animals) sets out what's known as the Five Freedoms, a framework designed to ensure the welfare of animals. And let me tell you, enrichment plays a massive role in ticking every single one of these boxes. Let's break it down. Freedom from hunger and thirst? Easy—think about food-based enrichment, like puzzle feeders, snuffle mats, or good old-fashioned scatter feeding. This makes mealtimes more engaging and taps into natural foraging instincts rather than just plonking a bowl down twice a day and calling it a job well done. Freedom from discomfort? Yep, that's covered too. By providing a varied environment—whether that's a cosy den for rest, different textures to walk on, or even cooling mats in the summer—you're making sure your dog is comfortable and not just stuck in the same old, uninspiring surroundings. Freedom from pain, injury, or disease? Now, while enrichment won't replace good veterinary care, it certainly prevents a whole heap of issues. Keeping a dog mentally stimulated reduces stress, and we all know that stress can lead to physical problems just as much as mental ones. Not to mention, controlled exercise and problem-solving activities help keep joints moving and brains sharp, which is particularly important as dogs age. Freedom to express normal behaviour? Well, this is where enrichment really shines. Dogs are meant to sniff, dig, chase, chew, problem-solve, and explore—these aren't "naughty" behaviours; they're normal behaviours that need an appropriate outlet. When we provide enrichment, we allow them to do what they were born to do, in a way that keeps both them and our furniture safe. And finally, freedom from fear and distress—another huge one. Enrichment builds confidence, provides mental stability, and helps prevent anxiety-related behaviours. A dog that has plenty of mental and physical engagement is a happy, well-adjusted dog who isn't living in a constant state of frustration or boredom. So, if you ever find yourself wondering whether enrichment is really *that* important, just remember this: it literally meets the gold standard of animal welfare. It's not just a luxury—it's a necessity. Plus, it makes life a whole lot more fun for both you and your dog, so why wouldn't you do it?

Chapter 21
Keeping Your Dog Sane (and You Too)
During Crate Rest & Restricted Exercise

I'm going to be honest, this chapter was a final thought before the book was sent off to be edited, and a request by my good friend Sara Barnes to add this chapter in. I do not like to disappoint, so here it is.

Let's be honest—if you've ever had a dog on crate rest or restricted exercise, you've probably experienced the sheer chaos that follows. Maybe it was after a neutering procedure, or something more serious like orthopaedic surgery, but whatever the reason, the minute you try to convince a dog that they need to rest, they look at you like you've lost the plot.

A doctor tells us humans, *"You need to rest,"* and for the most part, we nod and (eventually) comply—though I won't lie, even I've been guilty of ignoring medical advice in favour of *just cracking on.* But tell a dog to rest? Yeah, right. They don't have a clue what rest means. If anything, they wake up the day after surgery more full of beans than ever, bouncing off the walls, desperate to go for a walk, chase a ball, or do zoomies around the living room.

Back when I worked in vet practice, I used to get the same phone call over and over again the day after a dog's procedure.

"How do I keep my dog calm? He's dying to go for a walk!"

Some owners would break the rules, take the dog out anyway, and then— surprise, surprise—come back with complications. Others would sit crying into their cup of tea, wondering how on earth they were meant to stop their dog from bouncing around the house like a toddler on a sugar high. But here's the good news: You *can* keep your dog calm, and no, it doesn't involve sedating them or wrapping them in bubble wrap.

Dogs don't just need physical exercise; they need mental exercise too. If you give their brain something to do, they will be much more satisfied, which means they'll rest more and heal properly—and you won't have to spend the next two weeks wrestling them away from the front door.

Mental Stimulation: The Secret Weapon for Keeping Dogs Calm

When a dog is on crate rest or restricted exercise, they don't suddenly stop needing stimulation. They don't wake up and think, *Ah, I've had surgery, I'd better just sit here and reflect on life for a bit.* Instead, they feel exactly the same as they did before, only now they're trapped in a crate or limited to short toilet breaks, and they're wondering why you've suddenly turned into a prison warden.

The key is to give them something to do that keeps them engaged without overexerting them. Think of it as giving their brain a workout instead of their body. When I worked in practice, I'd suggest these little tricks to owners, and when they came back for their post-op check-ups, they'd tell me, "Oh my God, it worked! He's actually calm!"

So, what can you do?

First off, food-based enrichment is your best friend. If your dog is food-motivated, you can turn their meals into a game rather than just plonking a bowl down. Some of these exercises are repeated from previous chapters but are the better options to use for a dog on rest time. Try stuffing their food into a puzzle feeder, rolling it up in a towel for them to sniff out, or scattering it around a snuffle mat. If you don't have a fancy snuffle mat, don't worry—I've had great success with just hiding food in scrunched-up newspaper or inside cardboard boxes. It engages their natural sniffing and foraging instincts, making them feel like they've worked for their meal without moving much at all.

Another brilliant trick is the two-tea-towel game. Lay one tea towel flat, scatter some of your dog's kibble on it, then place another tea towel on top. Now let your dog sniff and nuzzle between the layers to find the food. It's low-impact, keeps them occupied, and doesn't involve them bouncing off the furniture like a lunatic.

If your dog isn't food-motivated, try scent work. Scent work is absolutely amazing for tiring dogs out without making them move too much. A simple way to do this is by grabbing a few old socks (preferably clean ones, unless you want to give your dog an extreme challenge), rubbing them with different scents (like herbs or dog-safe essential oils), and hiding them for your dog to find.

You can also make a DIY scent trail by dabbing a bit of chicken broth on a tissue and hiding it under something in the same room. Encourage your dog to use their nose to find it. Scent work is so mentally tiring that just ten minutes of it can drain more energy than a one-hour walk. And the best part? Your dog stays exactly where they should be—resting!

Another easy, low-impact game is "Find It." This is so simple but so effective. Take a handful of your dog's kibble or a few of their favourite treats, toss them onto a blanket, and let them sniff them out. Again, it satisfies their natural instincts without them needing to run, jump, or cause themselves a setback.

For dogs that enjoy problem-solving, try a plastic bottle puzzle. Take an empty plastic bottle, remove the cap, put some kibble inside, and let them figure out how to roll it around to get the food out. Just make sure they don't chew the bottle itself—some dogs will go *full gremlin mode* and try to eat the whole thing, which is not what we're aiming for here...we don't want any more visits to the vets.

Licky mats and frozen enrichment are also lifesavers. Smear some dog-safe peanut butter, natural yoghurt, or mashed banana onto a licky mat and freeze it. The licking motion itself is soothing for dogs, releases feel-good hormones, and helps them settle down. If you don't have a licky mat, just use a silicone baking mat or a plate—it works just as well.

For dogs who just want to be near you (but also need to be calm), interactive toy time can work wonders. Something as simple as gentle massage, slow-petting, or even watching TV together can help them settle. I've known dogs who will sit happily on crate rest watching nature documentaries, completely mesmerized. It's not a solution for every dog, but hey, if your dog wants to watch David Attenborough narrate the life cycle of a dung beetle, who am I to judge?

The trick with all of this is to rotate activities. If you try one thing and your dog loses interest, switch it up. Keep it varied, keep it interesting, and don't overthink it—dogs don't need high-tech gadgets to stay entertained; they just need something to engage their brain.

At the end of the day, dogs on crate rest don't understand why they can't go for a walk—but that doesn't mean they have to be bored out of their minds. If we can't exercise their bodies, we exercise their brains instead.

I've seen so many owners go from despair to relief when they realise that, yes, their dog *can* be calm after surgery. It just takes a little creativity, some patience, and a lot of food-stuffed toilet roll tubes.

So, if you're currently dealing with a dog on restricted exercise—take a deep breath, grab some snacks, and get creative. Because I promise you, the right kind of mental stimulation can make all the difference. And if nothing else, at least you won't have to deal with your dog staring at you like you've ruined their entire life for the next two weeks.

Chapter 22
My Day at the Zoo – Learning from the Best

At the very beginning of this book, I mentioned that I was planning a trip to Edinburgh Zoo to see how their enrichment team provides for the animals in their care. At the time of writing this final chapter in the book, I have literally just got back from the zoo, so I wanted to write this chapter while things were still fresh in my mind. And let me tell you—my day was not wasted. Not only did I rack up a ridiculous number of steps, but I got to dive deep into the world of enrichment at the highest level. We often talk about enrichment for dogs, but zoos have been doing this for years—long before the pet industry caught on. Their goal? To keep animals physically and mentally stimulated, prevent boredom, and allow them to express their natural behaviours. Sound familiar? Yep, just like dogs! This is what I have been badgering on about throughout the book.

One of the highlights of my trip was meeting Lucy Starbuck, an enrichment specialist at the zoo who primarily works with the chimpanzees. Now, when people hear the word *research* in the same sentence as *animals*, they often picture some dark, dodgy laboratory where animals are being injected, prodded, and generally having a miserable time. But that couldn't be further from the truth at Edinburgh Zoo. Zoos today are about conservation, education, and giving animals the best life possible—and the research they do here is purely cognitive. They want to understand just how intelligent these animals really are—and trust me, chimps are smart. Very smart.

At the zoo, chimps voluntarily participate in research by entering a special cognition centre. They can choose to engage in problem-solving tasks, and if they succeed, they get a tasty reward—usually one of their favourite foods. The centre is open daily between 9 am and 1 pm, and if the chimps want to enter, they can, and if they don't, that's also fine. No animal at the zoo is forced to do anything it doesn't want to, which I found incredible. Interestingly, similar tests are done with young children who visit the zoo to compare brain function and learning patterns between chimps and humans. Watching it in action, I couldn't help but wonder—who's actually smarter? Some of these chimps were solving problems quicker than I could (though to be fair, I was still digesting my full English breakfast at the time).

Hands-On with Chimp Enrichment (And My Rice Disaster)

One of the absolute best parts of my day was getting the chance to prepare some enrichment activities for the chimps myself. Now, I'd like to think I was born for this moment. I spend my life creating enrichment activities for dogs—how hard could it be? Turns out, I might need a little more practice.

We stuffed pipes with rice as a simple food puzzle, and the chimps—being the intelligent creatures they are—immediately started gathering sticks from their enclosure to poke through the pipes and retrieve the rice. Absolutely incredible to watch. Meanwhile, my first attempt at flinging food enrichment was a total disaster. I clearly hadn't stuffed the rice in tight enough because, instead of it landing nicely in the chimps' area, it exploded everywhere. It was a full-on rice explosion, with grains raining down like confetti. But hey ho, you live and learn, and the chimps certainly weren't complaining about the extra snacks.

Watching Animal Behaviours Up Close

Because I didn't have my kids with me this time (which, let's be honest, meant I wasn't spending half the day buying ice creams and making emergency toilet stops), I actually got to watch the animals properly—not just glance at them before getting dragged to the next enclosure. And let me tell you, observing the animals in detail was an absolute game-changer. I will add that I do enjoy taking the kids to the zoo, but yesterday was all about learning, and I made sure I didn't forget about them as I bankrupted myself at the gift shop for presents for them upon my return.

At the Warty Pig enclosure, I learned about the tiny population of these pigs in the wild—only around 200 left! Edinburgh Zoo holds nine of them, which makes up an incredible 4.5% of the world's population. That's wild (no pun intended). These pigs are incredibly intelligent, using sticks as tools to dig for food—something that not many people associate with pigs! It just goes to show that enrichment is crucial, whether you're working with a chimpanzee, a dog, or even a pig with an Elvis-inspired hairstyle (yes, that's a thing…you need to google warty pigs to see what I mean).

Next up, I sat in on a talk about armadillos. Did you know that armadillos have terrible eyesight but an amazing sense of smell? They actually rely more on their nose than their eyes to navigate and find food. That little fact made me think about how much we underestimate scent as enrichment—something I've banged on about throughout this book. And for those of you who love random animal facts, here's another one: some armadillos can breathe underground while digging. I don't know why, but that absolutely blew my mind.

The Link Between Zoo Enrichment and Dogs

Throughout my visit, one thing kept standing out—every single species needs enrichment. Whether it's a chimpanzee using tools, a warty pig rooting through the ground, or an armadillo sniffing out its next meal, they all require mental stimulation, problem-solving, and an outlet for their natural behaviours. And this is exactly the same for our dogs.

Lucy said something that really stuck with me: *"It doesn't matter if you are a dog, a chimpanzee, or even something as little as our stick insects here at the zoo—it's really important that we are providing animals with what they need. If we don't, they can become frustrated, and that's when you see a lot of unwanted* behaviours *."*

Sound familiar? This is exactly what happens with dogs when they don't get enough enrichment. They bark, they chew, they dig, they act out—not because they're 'bad' but because they have nowhere to channel their energy and instincts. By providing the right enrichment, we allow them to express natural behaviours in an appropriate way, and in doing so, we make their lives (and our lives) so much easier.

What We Can Learn From the Zoo

So, what did I take away from my visit? First of all, I got a lot of steps in, which was a win-win considering the size of my breakfast. But more importantly, I walked away with an even deeper appreciation for enrichment. Zoos have been doing this for years, and their entire goal is to ensure animals live enriched, fulfilling lives—even in captivity. That's exactly what we should be aiming for with our dogs.

Enrichment isn't a luxury—it's a necessity. Whether you're working with a highly intelligent chimp, an armadillo with a nose for adventure, or your pet dog who just wants to have a good time, the principle is the same: provide them with outlets for their natural behaviours, give them variety, and let them think.

I hope, after reading this book, you're walking away with the same mindset. Whether it's sniffing, solving puzzles, exploring new places, or engaging in creative activities, every bit of enrichment you provide makes your dog's world that much bigger and better. And if nothing else, remember this—if warty pigs can use tools and chimps can do cognitive puzzles, your dog is more than capable of tackling a toilet roll tube puzzle. So go forth, enrich their world, and have fun with it!

Bonus Section

I hope you have enjoyed reading this book, and I hope it has left you feeling motivated and ready to kickstart your dog's new enriched life. The best results come to those who take action and are patient with their dog. Remember, enrichment should be fun and not cause frustration.

I do appreciate that there is only so much you can take away from a book, which is why I have decided to share some free gifts with you.

- **My first gift to you is two months FREE access to The Sandancer Superhero Dog Club.**

Visit the Pets2impress website, www.pets2impress.com and sign up under the dog club section. Upon checkout, enter the code 9GAJMBTV to claim your two months free, and if you find it's not for you, then cancel at any time.

- **My second gift to you is a free download of the South Shields Dog-Friendly Map to start enriching your dog in new places**

Visit the link below to grab your copy

https://mailchi.mp/aa6c688ef631/your-dog-friendly-guide-to-south-shields

- **My third gift to you is a free PDF version of Recycle the**

Recycling, which will give you some ideas for some homemade brain games to use with your dog

Visit the link below to grab your copy

https://mailchi.mp/c877fefbe914/recycletherecycling

- **My fourth gift to you is a free webinar entitled, An Introduction to Scent Work**

Visit the link to watch the webinar

https://mailchi.mp/cc93605a09d7/an-introduction-to-scent-work

- **My Fifth gift to you is a free enrichment guide offering some additional ideas to try at home with your dog**

Visit the link below to grab your copy

https://mailchi.mp/3d8425d8a484/enrichment-guide

- **My sixth gift to you is a one I provided in one of my previous books, a little recipe book to help give you some inspiration in the kitchen for some yummy treats for your dog**

Visit the link below to grab your copy

https://mailchi.mp/79f391e0fb80/cakerecipes

· And my seventh gift to you is a free webinar all about enrichment that I delivered live to members of The Sandancer Superhero Dog Club.

Visit the link below to watch the webinar

https://mailchi.mp/9cc57b8a8f9f/free-enrichment-webinar

As a thank you for these invaluable gifts, please feel free to leave a glowing review on Amazon for me. If you make use of your two months FREE access to The Sandancer Superhero Dog Club, you will gain immediate access to my online courses, so be sure to sign up and get watching.

About The Author

Tim Jackson started his career working with animals as a veterinary auxiliary nurse. He trained and qualified as a veterinary nurse in 2007 at Myerscough College. He was promoted to Head Veterinary Nurse and spent a number of years helping animals and their owners.

In 2008, Tim launched Pets2impress, a company that took the region by storm. What began as a pet-sitting service soon expanded to offer a variety of services.

In 2014, Tim made the decision to leave his position as Head Veterinary Nurse to expand Pets2impress, a difficult decision but a necessary one to help expand and grow Pets2impress.

Tim has completed multiple animal behaviour courses, including the Think Dog Certificates and has a Diploma in Animal Behaviour. He passed each of these with distinction, and the knowledge he gained from these, combined with his extensive nursing experience, allowed him to offer one-on-one training sessions for all problem behaviours, utilizing only positive, reward-based training programmes.

This is a fun and stress-free method of training, which is easy to learn and rapidly achieves fantastic results. In its most basic form, it is a method of communication that is very clear for the dog. Examples of problem behaviours which Tim is able to assist with include separation anxiety, basic and foundation training, including lead and recall training, dog-on-dog aggression, and other anxiety-related issues. However, no problem is too small or too big for Tim.

In 2015, Tim opened a state-of-the-art enrichment-based daycare facility, offering a safe, enriching and stimulating environment for dogs whilst their owners are out at work. His experience as a qualified veterinary nurse, dog trainer, and canine behaviourist gave him a comprehensive understanding that all dogs have different physical and emotional needs, allowing daycare sessions to be tailor-made to suit each individual.

Tim runs his daycare as close to a nursery setting as possible and, therefore, follows a daily schedule as closely as possible. This is extremely beneficial to the dogs in his care as it has been well documented that dogs thrive off predictability, and it has positive effects on both their behaviour and mental wellbeing.

A typical day at the daycare centre includes controlled play, walks outside for a change of scenery, training time, top-to-tail examinations, and quiet time, as rest is extremely important to prevent overstimulation, which can have a negative impact on both behaviour and physical condition. In October 2019, Tim launched an additional package to the daycare service, the doggy 'adventure' daycare, to offer dogs further opportunities to receive physical and mental stimulation whilst in daycare, as well as receive the other benefits daycare has to offer. In June 2020, Tim launched two additional packages to the daycare service, The Scent Space and School Trips; as with the adventure daycares, these were designed to allow dogs further opportunities to receive physical and mental stimulation. In September 2020, Tim launched his brand-new unique daycare membership club, which is filled with so many benefits for owners and their dogs. Tim also launched picnics, and in 2023, Tim launched Magical Mondays at daycare and Forest School Fridays, as well as a brand-new Elite level on the daycare membership packages.

Tim is well known for his sense of humour and love and dedication to the welfare of all animals. Tim has owned several animals over the years, including a rescue tarantula (which he was absolutely terrified of), an iguana, bearded dragons, cats, hamsters, rats, mice, fish, and dogs.

Tim's mission in life is to help owners who struggle with their dogs, to save the dogs from ending up in shelters.

When not working, Tim can be seen swapping Doggy Daycare for Daddy Daycare. Tim loves nothing more than spending time with his four adorable children Sienna, Harvey, Darcey, and Alfie. He can also be found out walking his dogs Buddy and Bea and every now and then enjoys a nice pint at the local pub, although being an adult it takes around 3 months to organize anything with his friends.

Tim's **mission** statement at Pets2impress is:

"At Pets2impress, our mission is to provide a safe, enriching, and joyful environment for dogs to thrive. We are dedicated to offering a holistic daycare experience that fosters both mental and physical wellbeing through structured activities, personalised care, and a nurturing atmosphere. Our enrichment programs, including scent work, agility training, and adventurous outings, are designed to stimulate your dog's natural instincts and promote confidence, happiness, and overall health. We believe in creating a community where every dog feels valued and loved, ensuring they return home happier, healthier, and more balanced after each visit."

To find out more about Tim and Pets2impress please visit the Pets2impress website, www.pets2impress.com

Other Books by the Author

Available to purchase from www.pets2impress.com and Amazon

Help! My dog is a Devil with Other Dogs

Help! My dog doesn't like being left alone

Take the Lead for the Perfect Recall

The South Shields Puppy Playbook

Total Recall Training

Acknowledgments

As this is my sixth book, there are so many people I would like to thank, so many people who have supported me over the years and pushed me to always try harder. I definitely forgot to say thanks to certain people in my last five books, oops! I'll try harder in this book.

My first thanks must go to my adorable dogs that I have had over the years. It is thanks to them that I found my love for dog training and dog behaviour. Gone but never forgotten, I would like to dedicate this book to my first dog, Pip, Lady, Rosie, and my two current dogs, Buddy and Bea.

To my Mam and Dad, who are always there when I need them. I wouldn't be the person I am today without them.

A huge shoutout to my adorable children Sienna, Harvey, Darcey, and Alfie. They give me a purpose to continue working hard. I work hard to try and give them the life they deserve.

Special thanks to Shihan Mark Purcell and Sensei Blane Stamps, who have been so supportive during my karate journey and encouraged me to keep training hard. They truly are experts in the field of martial arts, and our club is lucky to have them.

A special shout out to Maureen, Neil, Lauren, and Sarah, who I met on holiday back in 2010. I am sure they thought they had seen the last of me when I got my flight home, but we have kept in touch over the years and I always enjoy a visit to Oldham to catch up. They are some of the nicest people I have ever met.

Special thanks to my good friend Annouska Muzyczuk, who has always stuck by me through thick and thin. She is one of my longest friends and the one person I turn to when I need help.

A special shout out to Chloe Boundy, whom I met when she completed her placement work at Pets2impress. I always enjoyed our pizza special Thursdays, but now enjoy our weeknights out for potato skins, garlic bread, and chocolate brownies. Chloe too has her very own successful dog-walking business.

A special shout out to Chriss Dodd and Jo Farrer, who I met at karate and have turned out to be two amazing friends over the years. It may take us three months to arrange a meet-up, but whenever we do, we always have a great laugh and put the world to rights.

To my mentor and Enrich University Business partner, Dominic Hodgson, the Pet Biz Wiz from Grow Your Pet Business Fast, for his guidance and support and for continuing to push me forward.

To members of The Elite Mastermind meeting I attend, thank you for your ongoing support and motivation and for being like a second family to me.

To the staff at Pets2impress: Naomi, Alicia, Kacey, Fiona, and Karen. 1. For putting up with me and for laughing at my not-so-funny jokes. 2. For your support, enthusiasm, and shared love you have for the dogs in our care. I couldn't do the job I do without my amazing team. 3. For going along with every crazy idea I have.

An additional super thank you to my team leader Naomi Brash for designing the cover of this book. She is way more tech-savvy than me and she never fails to impress me.

A special thanks to Joanna Hicklin for her amazing help with the Pets2impress Puppy School.

To my Pets2impress clients, who have been loyal to Pets2impress throughout the years. I would not be where I am today without your support, recommendations, and dedication. I am incredibly lucky to have such amazing clients who get involved with all the fun stuff we do here at daycare and in The Sandancer Superhero Dog Club.

An extra special thank you to members of the Sandancer Superhero Club who read this book prior to it being released. Jodie Wang from Real World Canine said: "Tim Jackson's passion for animals and their parents shines through in all he does. In many ways, he and I share the same objective: to keep dogs out of shelters. Tim has probably forgotten more about enrichment than most of us have yet to learn. This book offers great explanations on why enrichment is important and delves into how a dog's brain learns and works. Very very informative! You will not regret buying AND reading this book!"

To the veterinary staff who I used to work with for their support and recommendations over the years. They certainly had to put up with a lot from me, from singing constantly to winding each of them up on a daily basis. I certainly miss working with them every day.

My final thanks must go to you. Thank you for choosing this book and spending the time to read it. I hope you found it useful, and I hope you start to take action on the points made in this book. My mission is to try and prevent as many dogs from ending up in shelters as possible and to help dogs live happy, enriching lives. If this book helps others, then I can sleep well at night. I ask if you found this book useful that you leave a review on Amazon. I will accept no less than a 5-star rating.

Tim Jackson, RVNBCCSDip.Fda IMDTB

Made in the USA
Columbia, SC
29 June 2025

60085535R00067